HEINEMANN

SECONDARY

HISTORY

PROJECT

# MEDICINE THROUGH TIME

## Nigel Kelly • Bob Rees • Paul Shuter

Heinemann

Heinemann Educational Publishers

Halley Court, Jordan Hill, Oxford OX2 8EJ
Part of Harcourt Education
Heinemann is a registered trademark of
Harcourt Education Limited

**Tel: 01865 888058  www.heinemann.co.uk**

Teacher support material and activities for students are available for
this title at www.heinemann.co.uk/medicine.

You will need to use a password to gain access to this material. The
passwords are :

for material to support the *core edition* of this book : **core**
for material to support the *foundation edition* of this book : **foundation**

Designed by Ken Vail Graphic Design

Illustrated by Arthur Phillips

Printed in Italy by Printer Trento Srl

Cover design by The Wooden Ark Studio

**Photographic acknowledgements**

The authors and publisher would like to thank the following for
permission to reproduce photographs:

Ancient Art and Architecture Collection: 1.1A, 5.3I; Ann Ronan Picture
Library: 8.5I, 9.4Q; Antonia Reeve/Science Photo Library: 12.3O;
Australian Aboriginal Cultures Gallery, South Australian Museum:
1.4E; Bibliotheque Nationale Paris: 7.4F, 13.1B; Bodleian Library: 9.1A;
Bridgeman Art Library/Private Collection: 11.5O; Bridgeman Art
Library: 2.2A; Bridgeman Art Library/Musee de L'Hotel Sandelin: 9.6
(1); Bridgeman Art Library/York City Art Gallery: 9.5T; British
Library Reproductions: 8.4G, 8.6O; British Museum Library: 4.6I, 5.6
(2), 9.2G; BSIP, Edwige/Science Photo Library: 12.3N; C.M. Dixon:
3.1A, 3.2B, 4.1A, 5.3H; Cambridge University Library: 8.2D; Centre for
the Study of Cartoons, University of Kent: 13.4X; Chester Beatty
Library, Dublin/Cumulus: 7.2A; Coo.ee Historical Picture Archive:
1.4F; Corbis Bettman/UPI: 12.2L; Count Robert Begouen, Musee
Pujol, France: 1.2C; E.T. Archive: 4.6K, 12.1A; Francesca Countway
Library: 12.1C; Frank Graham: 5.3G; Hildesheim Museum: 2.3C;
Hulton Deutsch Collection: 11.3J, 12.3 (p.113), 12.5 (p.119 bottom), 13.2
(p.126); Hulton-Deutsch Collection/Corbis: 13.4 (p.135); Imperial War
Museum: 12.3 (p.110); Jean-Loup Charmet/Science Photo Library:
11.4M; Louvre Ager: 4.7L; Mansell Collection: 10.1B, 12.4S, 13.2G;
Mary Evans Picture Library: 8.3F, 10.1 (p.77 top), 11.1 (p.81), 11.1C,
11.2I, 11.3 (p.86), 11.5 (p.90), 12.5 (p.119 top right), 13.5 (2); Michael
Holford: 4.3F, 5.3E; Musee Pasteur: 11.3 (p.85), 11.7 (1); National
Portrait Gallery: 13.3 (p.129 left); Paul Shuter: 5.3 (p.35); Punch: 13.3P,
13.3S, 13.3T, 13.4Z; Robert Harding: 7.3C, 12.3M; Ronald
Sheridan/Ancient Art and Architecture Collection: 4.2D; Royal
College of Surgeons: 10.1 (p.77 bottom), 10.1A; Science & Society
Picture Library: 11.5 (p.93); Science Photo Library/St Mary's Hospital:
11.5Q, 11.5T; Science Photo Library: 11.7 (5), 12.1G, 12.5 (p.119 top left),
13.3 (p.129 right); The Art Archive/Bardo Museum Tunis/Dagli Orti:
5.6 (3); Timepix/Rex/Mansell Collection: 13.1D; Trinity College,
Cambridge: 8.6M; University of Bradford, Calvin Wells Collection:
1.3D; Wellcome Institute Library: 2.5I, 4.2C, 12.1F, 12.2J, 12.4X, 13.2H,
13.2J, 13.5 (1); Werner Forman Archive: 12.4W; West Stowe Country
Park: 6D; Zentrale Farbbild Agentur: 9.1B

Cover photo: © Royal College of Surgeons

**Written source acknowledgements**

The authors and publisher gratefully acknowledge the following
publications from which sources in the book have been drawn. In
some sources the wording or sentence structure has been simplified:

P. Addison A New Jerusalem (Cape, 1985): 13.3U; P. Addison Now the
War is Over (Cape, 1985): 13.4Y; M. Alexander Earliest English Poems
(Penguin, 1966): 6A; R.A. Browne British Latin Selections, AD500-1400
(Blackwell, 1954): 8.7Y; J. Chadwick, W.N. Mann, I.M. Ionie and E.T.
Withington Hippocratic Writings (Penguin, 1983): 4.3G; M.W Flynn
(ed.) A Report of the Sanitary Conditions of the Labouring Population
of Great Britain (Edinburgh University Press, 1965): 13.2K, 13.2M;
GLC A History of the Black Presence in London (GLC, 1986): 12.4U;
The Guardian (27/6/2001): 12.5Y; D. Guthrie A History of Medicine
(Nelson, 1945): 8.5J; W.O. Hassall They Saw it Happen 55BC-1485
(Blackwell, 1956): 6B; K. Haeger The Illustrated History of Surgery
(Harold Starke, 1988): 12.1D; W.H.S. Jones Pliny's Natural History
(Heinemann, 1923): 5.6 (3); G. Keynes The Apology and Treatise of
Ambrose Pare (Falcon Educational Books, 1951): 9.3J, 9.3K, 9.3L, 9.3M;
H. Lloyd Jones The Greek World (Penguin, 1965): 5.6 (1); M.V. Lyons
Medicine in the Medieval World (Macmillan, 1984): 8.2B, 8.2C, 8.5K;
A. McIntosh Gray Medical Care and Public Health: 1780 to the Present
Day (OUP, 1990): 11.5U, 11.5V; R.H. Major Classic Descriptions of
Disease (Charles S. Thompson, 1945): 8.7S, 8.7V, 8.7W; V. Nutton 'A
Social History of Graeco-Roman Medicine' in Medicine in Society
(CUP, 1994): 5.2B; E.D. Phillips Greek Medicine (Thames and Hudson,
1975): 4.5H, 4.6J; C. Platt The English Medieval Town (Granada, 1979):
8.6N; D. Poynter History at Source: Medicine 300-1929 (Evans
Brothers, 1971): 11.5 (4); R. Reid Microbes and Men (BBC, 1974): 11.7
(2&3), 12.2I; P. Rhodes An Outline of the History of Medicine
(Butterworths, 1985): 12.4T; M. Ridley Disease (Pheonix, 1997): 11.6Y;
SCHP Medicine Through Time: A Study in Development Book 1
(Holmes McDougal, 1976): 8.7P, 8.7Q, 8.7R; SCHP Medicine Through
Time: A Study in Development Book 3 (Holmes McDougal, 1976):
13.2N; J. Scott Medicine Through Time (Holmes McDougal, 1987):
11.1G; R. Shyrock The Development of Modern Medicine (London,
1984): 12.6 (2); C. Singer and E.A. Underwood A Short History of
Medicine (OUP, 1962): 4.7M; C. Singer Galen On Anatomical
Procedures (London, 1956): 5.5K, 9.2C; J.D. de C.M. Saunders and
C.D. O'Malley The Illustrations for the Works of Andreas Vesalius
(World Publishing, 1950): 9.2D; G. Sweetman A History of Wincanton
(London and Wincanton, 1903): 11.1D; L. Thorndike Michael Scot
(Nelson, 1965): 8.3E; R. Vallery-Radot Life of Pasteur (London, 1911):
11.2H; J.J. Walsh Medieval Medicine (London, 1920): 6C; L. M.
Zimmerman and I Veith Great Ideas in the History of Surgery
(London, 1961): 12.2K

# CONTENTS

## CHAPTER 1 PREHISTORIC MEDICINE

## CHAPTER 2 EGYPTIAN MEDICINE

## CHAPTER 3 MINOAN CRETE

## CHAPTER 4 ANCIENT GREECE

## CHAPTER 5 ROMAN MEDICINE

## CHAPTER 6 THE FALL OF THE ROMAN EMPIRE IN THE WEST

## CHAPTER 7 ISLAMIC MEDICINE

# PREHISTORIC MEDICINE

## 1.1 What was the prehistoric period?

For historians, a prehistoric society is one without writing. Although the prehistoric period does not have a definitive starting point and finishing point, historians usually say it started about 500,000 years ago. All of the evidence we are studying, however, comes from the last 20,000 years.

Prehistoric people lived throughout the world. Not all peoples in the world left the prehistoric period at the same time. Once writing developed in a society, that society was no longer prehistoric. So Britain was still prehistoric long after Egypt and the Middle East, where writing developed much earlier.

The earliest prehistoric peoples had the following features in common.

- They were nomads.
- They were hunter gatherers – so they got all their food without farming.
- They lived in small groups without complicated political arrangements. There were no separate countries.
- They had a very simple level of technology – spears, bows and arrows, axes, knives and scrapers were their main tools. All of these were made from wood, bone and stone.
- They had no system of writing.

Over thousands of years things changed slowly. The most important changes were the development of farming (which meant people stayed in one place) and metal tools.

**Source A**

▲ A cave painting made by prehistoric people in France about 15,000 years ago.

## QUESTIONS

1 Look at each of the common features of early prehistoric peoples listed on this page.

a Explain the feature.

b How do you think it might have affected the medicine they used, and our ability to find out about their medicine?

| Old Stone Age | | | | New Stone Age | | Bronze Age | Iron Age |
|---|---|---|---|---|---|---|---|
| 18000 BC | 15000 BC | 12000 BC | 9000 BC | 6000 BC | 3000 BC | 0 | AD 2000 |

Cave paintings in France
Sources A and C

▲ **The Stone Age (in most of Europe and the Middle East).**

We can tell that prehistoric people suffered injury and disease. Their bones show us this. What we do not know, however, is if, or how, they treated themselves.

## Source B

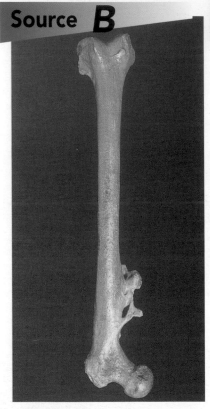

▲ The thigh bone of a prehistoric person. You can clearly see a large growth on the bone.

## Source C

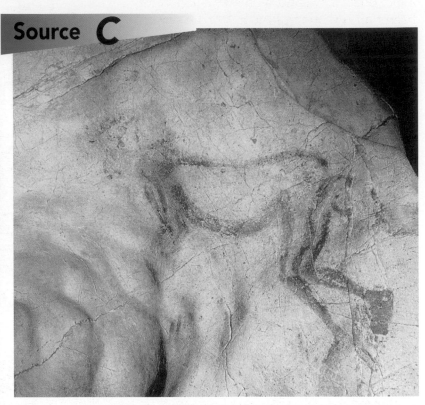

▲ A cave painting made by prehistoric people in France about 15,000 years ago. We cannot be sure exactly what this painting shows, but many other prehistoric paintings show a man with antlers like this one, often standing in a circle with twelve other men.

▶ This modern drawing of the cave painting in Source C shows the outline of a man with antlers, possibly wearing a mask, more clearly.

# 1.3 Trephined skulls: a prehistoric operation

Trephined skulls have been found in almost every part of the world where prehistoric people lived. Trephining is when a hole is cut in a person's skull while they are still alive. Both men's and women's skulls have been found with trephine holes, but never a child's skull. They are found in burial sites with the complete body of the person. Often the piece of bone that was cut out of the skull was found in the grave with the body. Often this piece of skull had one or two holes made in it, perhaps so it could have been threaded on a thong and worn round the neck. Most of the skulls have bone growth around the hole made by the operation. This means that these persons lived on, probably for many years. Historians have to work out why this operation, which must have been both painful and dangerous, was done. These are the main theories historians have put forward since these skulls were first found in the 1860s:

**Theory 1:** Dr Prunieres (1865) suggested the holes were made in the skulls so they could be used as drinking vessels.

**Theory 2:** Professor Paul Broca (1876) suggested the operation was performed on children, and those who survived were thought to have great magic power. When the person died, the skull and the piece taken out were used as very powerful charms.

**Theory 3:** E. Guiard (1930) suggested trephining operations were originally performed on people who had skull injuries and, later, on people with other problems, perhaps epilepsy or very bad headaches.

**Theory 4:** Douglas Guthrie (1945) suggested that the operation may have been performed to let evil spirits out of the body.

## QUESTIONS

1 Look at sources B–D. For each source

  a Say whether it is *definitely* evidence that prehistoric people suffered from disease.

  b Say whether it tells us anything about how prehistoric people treated disease.

2 We can be sure that some of the theories about trephining given on this page are wrong as they are contradicted by the evidence. Some of them may be right or they may not – we cannot be sure. Look at each theory in turn.

  a Describe the theory.

  b Say whether you think the theory is definitely wrong, could be right or wrong, or is definitely right.

  c Explain why the evidence of the sources supports your answer to part **b**.

**Source D**

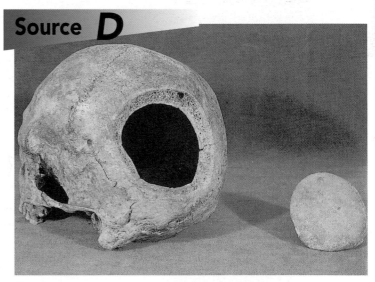

▲ A skull of a prehistoric adult found, in 1938, at Crichel Down in Dorset. The hole in the skull was cut out while the person was alive. They probably lived for many years after the operation because the bone grew a little where it was cut – rounding off the edge. The disc of bone that was cut out of the skull was buried with the person.

## Historians and evidence

Historians have a real problem interpreting the evidence about prehistoric medicine. We know some facts. There was illness. Trephining operations were performed. We do not know what people thought about illness though, and we do not know why trephining operations were done. To help provide explanations, historians have looked at the medical beliefs of various groups around the world whose technology and lifestyle are similar to prehistoric people.

The Aborigines of central and southern Australia were visited by anthropologists during the late 19th and early 20th centuries. Before these visits, the Aborigines had little or no contact with the European settlers in Australia. The Aborigines lived in the harsh conditions of the Australian desert. They obtained their food by hunting and by gathering wild plants. They were nomads, moving from water hole to water hole. They had many spoken languages but no written one. In all these ways they were very similar to prehistoric people.

## Aboriginal spirits

The Aborigines thought the world started in the dreamtime when the spirit ancestors lived. Many things in their world were hard to explain – why was there a stream or a water hole in one place and not another? Their answer was because the spirit ancestors had put one there. Spirits were also thought to be the cause of new life – whether human or animal. Anything which did not have an obvious physical explanation was explained as the work of spirits.

## The causes of illness

This division, between things with an obvious cause and things without an obvious cause, was part of aboriginal medicine. Some problems were treated with common-sense cures:

- Broken arms were encased in clay which would set hard in the sun – very like a modern plaster cast.
- Cuts were covered with clay or animal fat and bound up with bark or animal skin.

Other problems did not have an obvious cause. Aborigines had two explanations for these. The first was that an evil spirit had entered the sick person's body. The second was that the person's own spirit had left, or been taken, from his or her body. If an enemy had captured the sick person's spirit with a pointing bone (see page 9), then the treatment was to try and find the bone, which would have the spirit stuck to it. If the illness was thought to be caused by an evil spirit in the person's body then the treatment would try to drive that spirit out. This gives us an important insight into the history of medicine. The cures people used were related to what they thought caused the disease. If the disease was thought to have a spiritual cause, then only a spiritual cure would make sense.

## THE PREHISTORIC PERIOD

Historians divide the prehistoric period into a number of different eras:

**Old Stone Age** (Palæolithic) when people were nomadic hunter gatherers.

**New Stone Age** (Neolithic) when farming and living in one place became common.

**Bronze Age** when metal tools were first used.

**Iron Age** when the new metal greatly improved the tools and weapons which could be made.

There was an overlap in time between the prehistoric period and those described in the next chapters. Most of Europe was in the New Stone Age during the height of the Egyptian civilization. The Minoan civilization happened at the same time as the Bronze Age in other places, and Britain was in the Iron Age during the Greek and early Roman periods.

▲ An Aboriginal healing amulet. Amulets were tied over painful parts of the body. This one is made of shrub fibres and emu feathers.

▲ These Aborigines are chanting and pointing a special 'death bone', which they believed gave them the power to kill from a distance.

## QUESTIONS

1  In what ways were 19th century Aborigines like prehistoric people?

2  a  Describe an Aboriginal common-sense treatment.

   b  Why do you think they did not use a spirit cure for this treatment?

3  a  Describe an Aboriginal spiritual treatment.

   b  Why do you think they did not use a common-sense treatment for this problem?

4  Do you think Aborigines would use spiritual or common-sense treatments for the following problems?

   a  A sprained wrist caused in a fall.

   b  A heart attack.

   c  An epileptic fit.

   d  A spear wound.

   Explain the reasons for your answer in each case.

## 1.5 Conclusions

The 19th century aboriginal way of life was very similar to what we know about the way of life of prehistoric people. The ideas of the aborigines may therefore help us understand the ideas of prehistoric people. If the aborigines used both common sense and a belief in spirits in their medicine, so might prehistoric people. The man shown in Source C (page 6) may have been a medicine man. The medicine man's (or woman's) explanation for many illnesses may have been that they were caused by evil spirits. Trephining operations may have been performed to let out evil spirits through the hole in the skull. The pieces of skull removed in the operation may have been worn as a charm to keep evil spirits away. This is the view of prehistoric medicine that historians think is most likely. However, it is only a theory. Because we have no written records from prehistoric times, we cannot be sure what people really thought.

The chart below summarizes the important information about prehistoric medicine. There is one of these charts for each chapter in the first half of the book. Completing the chart is a useful way to look back over the material you have just studied, to make sure you understand it. Correctly filled in charts will be useful for revision. Notice how many of the sections of the chart have a place for *Evidence*. Good historians can always support what they say with evidence and so should you when you take exams. Filling in these sections of the chart will give you useful practice in selecting the facts which you can use to back up answers.

The chart is split into four different sections:

*Factors affecting Medicine* which is explained in more detail on the right.

*Causes of Disease* which is concerned with what people thought caused disease at the time.

*Treatments Used* where you can record some of the ways in which injury and diseases were treated.

*New Features* where you need to think about each period in relation to the ones which went before.

## Factors affecting Medicine

This section is about the factors that have influenced change and development. The most important factors are:

*Science and/or Technology* For example, our highly developed science and technology, with x-rays and ultrasound helps medicine because it allows doctors to discover what is happening inside the body.

*War* For example, plastic surgery was developed during World War Two to help air crew with new and terrible burns.

*Religion* For example, some religious groups today do not allow blood transfusions.

*Government* and the way society is organized and run. For example, the creation of the National Health Service and state funded medicine in Britain in 1948.

*Communications* from the development of writing to air transport. For example, modern transplants are often only possible because organs can be flown from one hospital to another.

*Chance*, unplanned events. For example, penicillin was first found when Alexander Fleming was checking through the remains of old and failed experiments.

**Copy and complete the summary chart below.**

| Prehistoric Medicine | | | | | |
|---|---|---|---|---|---|
| **Factors affecting Medicine** | | **Causes of Disease** | | **New Features** | |
| Factor | Effect | Cause | Evidence | Feature | Evidence |
| 1_____ | No method of writing so difficult to preserve knowledge or pass it on accurately so progress difficult. | 1 Supernatural:<br>a) Loss of a person's spirit<br>b) Evil spirit in the body | _____ | 1 Spirits thought to cause disease. | |
| 2_____ | An unstable society, large scale projects and long term planning almost impossible so progress difficult. | 2 Physical:<br>simple injuries like a broken arm or leg | _____ | 2 Medicine men or women – special people to treat the sick. | a) Aborigines<br>b) _____ |

| Treatments Used | | |
|---|---|---|
| Treatment | Illness | Evidence |
| 1 _____ | Cannot be sure | Skulls (Source D) |
| 2 Encased in clay | _____ | Aborigines |
| 3 Covered with clay or animal fat and bound with bark or animal skin. | Cuts | _____ |
| 4 _____ | Any disease without an obvious physical cause. | Aborigines |

| 3_____ | No understanding of how the body worked so progress difficult. |
|---|---|

| 3 Magical cures | a) _____<br>b) _____ |
|---|---|
| 4 Common sense cures | Aborigines |

# CHAPTER 2

# EGYPTIAN MEDICINE

## 2.1 Ancient Egypt

### Life in Ancient Egypt

The Ancient Egyptian civilization lasted for about 2600 years, from around 3000 BC to about 400 BC. Egypt was a well-organized and hierarchical society, from the pharaoh and the vizier at the top, to the peasants who worked the land at the bottom. The physical geography of the country forced people to settle along the banks of the river Nile. The Nile flooded once a year. This kept the surrounding land very fertile. Successful farming of this land left the Egyptians time for other things. They developed into a specialized society. There were priests, scribes, lawyers and doctors, as well as craftsmen like the stonemasons and painters who made the great buildings. Sons were trained by their fathers from an early age in the same job. In some professions, including medicine, a father might train his daughter to do his job if he had no sons.

The most important difference between the Egyptians and prehistoric people was that the Egyptians had developed writing. The development of writing affected their medicine. It meant they could write about illnesses and treatments, and so keep a record of those treatments that worked and those that did not. This enabled them to develop their treatments by trial and error.

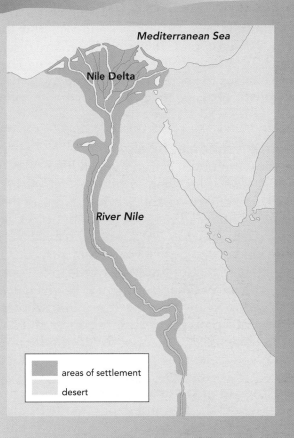

### Egyptian religion

The Egyptians were very religious and believed in many gods. These gods made everything happen, from the rising of the sun to the flooding of the river Nile each year, without which the Egyptians would not have been able to grow crops. Some of these gods were thought to cause and cure disease. The goddess of war, Sekhmet, was also thought to cause and cure epidemics. Thoth is described in a medical book, the *Papyrus Ebers*, as the god who 'gives physicians the skill to cure'.

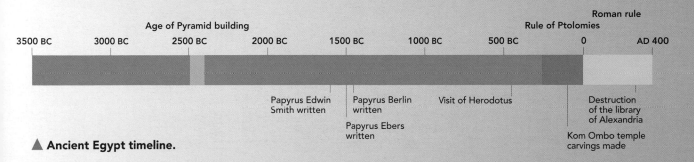

▲ Ancient Egypt timeline.

Because the Egyptians left written records, we know what they thought caused illnesses and also how they treated them. The Egyptians believed that many diseases were caused by an evil spirit entering the body. They often wore charms to keep these spirits away. If they became ill despite the charms, they turned to magic and the gods to make them well.

### Egyptian medical books

The most important early Egyptian medical books were the *Books of Thoth*. They were kept by his priests in the temple of Thoth, god of writing and wisdom. None of these books have survived but a medical book from about 1500 BC that has survived, the *Papyrus Ebers*, was probably based on them. These kind of books give very clear instructions on how to treat illness. This includes the exact words to be spoken as well as any medicine or other treatment to be given. Doctors were supposed to follow the procedure outlined precisely. If a doctor followed the procedures and the patient still died, the doctor was not blamed. If, however, the doctor did not follow the book precisely and the patient died, the doctor was executed.

### Treatments and cures

The first herbal cures and drugs (made from minerals, herbs and animal parts) were probably given as part of the magical cure, not as an alternative to magic. They were intended to drive the evil spirit away, perhaps because of their smell or bitter taste. Drugs were either boiled and strained, or pounded to a fine powder. They were then mixed up and given with wine, water or beer. They were sometimes mixed into pills with dough, or mixed with honey. Chest diseases were often treated by making the patient inhale steam. Wounds and skin conditions were treated with ointments. Many of the Egyptians' drugs are still used, in a different form, in medicines today. Their record keeping shows that, if a remedy worked, they kept using it. The Egyptians' faith in these remedies would probably have been as much to do with their belief in magic as their faith in a particular drug.

## Source A

▲ An amulet of the goddess Taweret. Taweret, a pregnant hippopotamus, was the goddess of childbirth. Taweret's face is shown looking fierce to drive away evil spirits which might affect either the mother or the baby. These amulets were worn by pregnant women to keep themselves safe during pregnancy and childbirth, which, for them, was a very dangerous time.

▶ A spell from the *Papyrus Ebers*. The doctor was to chant this spell while giving the patient the medicine. The Egyptian doctor who used the papyrus had written next to the spell, 'This spell is really excellent – successful many times.' The *Papyrus Ebers* was made about 1500 BC.

## Source B

Here is the great remedy. Come! You who drive evil things from my stomach and my limbs. He who drinks this shall be cured just as the gods above were cured.

## QUESTIONS

1 What were the main differences between life in Ancient Egypt and prehistoric times?

2 Why are Egyptian medical books important to historians of medicine?

3 What do the *Books of Thoth* and the *Papyrus Ebers* tell us about what the Egyptians thought caused disease?

## EGYPTIAN MEDICAL BOOKS

Only a few medical books have survived from Ancient Egypt. They were written on papyrus, a kind of paper made from reeds. The books we know about have been found by archaeologists. They are known by the name of the modern owner, or museum where they are kept. The *Papyrus Edwin Smith* was bought by Smith, an American egyptologist, in 1862. It was written about 1600 BC and considers wounds and the work of surgeons as well as treatments and drugs. The *Papyrus Ebers*, written about 1500 BC, contains over 700 remedies. It is named after a German egyptologist, Maurice Ebers, who acquired it in 1873. The *Papyrus Berlin*, owned by the Berlin Museum, was written about 1450 BC, and concentrates on the treatment and protection of mothers and babies.

# 2.3 Religion and anatomy

Anatomy is the study of the structure of the body. Knowing how the body is made up, and how it works, is an important part of medicine. The Egyptians learned some anatomy as an unintended consequence of their religious beliefs. They believed that after a person died, his or her soul left the body. After a while the soul returned to the body and the person then began an afterlife, very like the life they had led before they died. It was important, therefore, to keep dead bodies in good condition for their souls to use when they returned.

## Source D

Forty-six vessels go from the heart to every limb. If a doctor, surgeon or exorcist places his hands or fingers on the back of the head, hands, stomach, arms or feet, then he hears the heart. The heart speaks out of every limb.

▲ From the *Papyrus Ebers*, about 1500 BC.

## Source C

▲ Parts of the mummification process from a painted coffin from around 600 BC. The lower section shows the body (darker in colour than the living people) being washed in a natron (sodium chloride) solution. The middle section shows the body covered with natron crystals during the 40 day drying-out stage. At the top, on the left, the mummy has been placed in its tomb with the *canopic* jars underneath. They held the liver, lungs, stomach and intestines. On the right the god Anubis is attending to the mummy.

The Egyptians devoted much time to finding out ways of preserving bodies. They soaked the bodies in various liquids, including salts and bitumen. They covered them in oils and wrapped them in bandages. This process was called embalming, and the embalmed bodies were called mummies.

Embalming included cutting open the body to take out the main organs (heart, lungs, liver, spleen, brain) because they would rot. They were kept whole and stored with the mummy in canopic jars. The process of embalming gave the Egyptians a good understanding of some parts of human anatomy. Removing the major organs meant they knew where they were located inside the body. But their belief in the afterlife, which meant that they carried out the embalming in the first place, prevented them from doing any further research into the structure of the body. Because the body was needed for the afterlife it could not be further dissected.

## Source E

In the best treatment, first of all they draw out the brains through the nostrils with an iron hook. When they have removed what they can in this way they flush out the remainder with drugs. Next they make a cut in the side, with an obsidian knife, through which they take out all the internal organs. They clean out the body cavity, rinsing it with palm wine and powdered spices, and then they stitch it up again. When they have done this, they cover the corpse in natron for 70 days and so mummify it. Then they wash the corpse and wrap it from head to toe in linen bandages smeared with the finest gum. Finally the relatives put it in a man-shaped wooden coffin and store it in a burial chamber, where it is propped upright against the wall. This is the most costly method of preparing the dead.

▲ A description of one of the methods of mummification from *The Histories*, a book written by Herodotus, a Greek traveller and historian who visited Egypt about 450 BC.

# 2.4 A natural theory of the causes of disease

The river Nile was vital to Egyptian life. Every year the river flooded. Its waters were dammed and channelled into irrigation ditches to keep the crops growing. This control of the flood waters by damming gave some doctors an alternative theory about the cause of disease. They thought the human body might be full of channels, rather like the irrigation system. Their knowledge of anatomy told them that there were many vessels inside the body through which blood and other fluids flowed. If an irrigation channel got blocked, the life giving water would not flow into the fields. Perhaps the same thing happened inside the human body? If one of the vessels became blocked would the person become ill?

This was a very different idea about the causes of disease from those held earlier.

Now the disease was believed to have a physical as well as a spiritual cause. That meant the treatment should include the physical as well. These Egyptian doctors used a variety of treatments:

- Vomiting was thought to be good for some patients. It might clear blockages in some parts of the body.
- Purges (medicines that worked as laxatives), were often used. They might clear some blockages from the stomach and bowel.
- Bleeding was also used. A doctor would deliberately cut a vein so that the patient lost a certain amount of blood. This, it was thought, might clear any blockages in the blood vessels.

These methods were not accepted by everyone, nor did doctors who used them reject spiritual explanations for disease. The treatments in the *Papyrus Ebers* show both the **natural** and the **supernatural** theories of the causes of disease.

## Source F

There are two vessels in the arm. If he is ill in his arm then let him vomit by means of fish and beer and bandage his fingers with water melon until he is healed. If he is ill in the bowel the blockage must be cleared. **Colocynth**, senna, fruit of sycamore are ground together into a paste and shaped into four cakes for him to eat.

▲ **Treatment from the *Papyrus Ebers*, about 1500 BC.**

# 2.5 Surgery

Surgery, like all crafts in Egypt, was passed on from father to son (or sometimes daughter). The *Papyrus Edwin Smith*, written in about 1600 BC, describes some simple surgical procedures, including treating dislocated arms and legs. None of the existing written records discuss major operations nor do the mummies that have so far been examined show any signs of major surgery.

On the other hand, as we have seen, the Egyptians had a reasonable grasp of human anatomy. The written evidence shows that they performed minor surgery, like the removal of cysts and tumours. Because so much surgery was done, it was likely that it was one of the medical skills in which people specialized. These minor operations probably had quite a good recovery rate, because the wounds that were left after operating were treated with willow. We now know that willow leaves and bark produce a form of antiseptic, which would have protected the wound against infection.

## Source G

If you examine a man with a dislocation of his jaw where his mouth is open and he cannot close it, you should put your two thumbs on the ends of the two rami of the mandible [lower jawbone] inside the mouth. Put your fingers under his chin and make them fall back into the correct position.

▲ **From the *Papyrus Edwin Smith*, about 1600 BC.**

## Source H

When you come across a swelling of the flesh in any part of the body of the patient and your patient is clammy and the swelling comes and goes under your finger unless the finger is still, then you must say to your patient, 'It is a tumour of the flesh. I will treat the disease. I will try to heal it with fire since cautery heals.' When you come across a swelling that has attacked a vessel, then it has formed a tumour in the body. If, when you examine it with your fingers, it is like a hard stone, then you should say, 'It is a tumour of the vessels. I shall treat the disease with a knife.'

▲ **From the *Papyrus Ebers*, about 1500 BC.**

## Source I

◄ **Egyptian surgical instruments carved in the temple of Kom Ombo in around 100 BC. They include probes, saws, forceps, flasks, scalpels, scissors and even plants (presumably medicinal herbs to put on the wound after surgery to help it heal). Surgical instruments were mostly made from bronze, although the Egyptians used flint knives for circumcision, which had both religious and ceremonial importance.**

# Egyptian public health

The Egyptians believed in keeping clean. It seems that their concern with cleanliness was more to do with religion and comfort than with health. The fact that priests washed more often than other people suggests a religious connection for their washing practices. Their development of mosquito nets was more to do with comfort than the knowledge of the illnesses that mosquitoes can carry. But, whatever their reasons, their attitude to cleanliness helped them to keep healthy. Shaven heads were normal, for both men and women. Clothes were changed regularly.

Despite their sophisticated water drainage system for growing crops the Egyptians do not seem to have developed a drainage system for their toilets. Only well-off people had bathrooms and the baths were just shallow troughs with a drainage pipe leading to a large jar. Toilets were more common, but these were just stone seats over a large removable jar. Perhaps this shows that water was too valuable to be wasted in deep baths or used for sluicing away sewage, which could be carried to the fields by slaves and used as manure.

▲ An artist's reconstruction of an Egyptian toilet seat made of limestone.

## Source J

The Egyptians drink from cups of bronze which they clean daily – everyone, without exception. They wear linen clothes which they make a special point of continually washing. Their priests shave their whole bodies every third day, to guard against lice, or anything else equally unpleasant while they do their religious duties. Twice a day and every night these priests wash in cold water.

▲ From *The Histories* by the Greek historian Herodotus, about 450 BC.

## QUESTIONS

Copy the following statements about Egyptian medicine and underline them. Underneath each statement:

a Give some evidence to support it and explain why the evidence supports it.

b Explain whether it is a new or an old idea in the history of medicine.

1 Where there was no obvious physical cause for disease some Egyptian doctors thought disease was caused by spirits and gods.

2 Egyptian doctors knew something about anatomy. They were aware of the heart, lungs, and brain.

3 Egyptian doctors used treatments based on herbs, plants and animal parts.

4 Some Egyptian doctors thought the body was like the river Nile with channels running through it. If the channels got blocked, a person would become ill.

5 Many Egyptians thought the best way to stay healthy was to scare away the evil spirits that might cause disease, so they wore charms to help them do this.

6 Egyptians were very concerned about their personal hygiene and this helped protect their health.

7 Some Egyptian doctors gave their patients careful physical examinations.

8 Egyptian doctors treated wounds, dislocations, and tumours.

Study the sources below and then answer the questions.

## Source 1

**EXAMINATION**
If you examine a man whose nose is disfigured – part being squashed in, while the other part is swollen and both his nostrils are bleeding.
**DIAGNOSIS**
Then you should say, 'You have a broken nose and this is something I can treat'.
**TREATMENT**
You should clean his nose with two plugs of linen and then insert two plugs soaked in grease in his nostrils. You should make him rest until his swelling has gone down, you should bandage his nose with stiff rolls of linen and treat him with lint every day until he recovers.

▲ From the *Papyrus Edwin Smith*, written in about 1600 BC.

## Source 2

These words are to be spoken over the sick person: 'Oh spirit, male or female, who lurks hidden in my flesh and my limbs, get out of my flesh! Get out of my limbs!'

▲ From the *Papyrus Berlin*, written in about 1450 BC.

**Copy and complete the summary chart below.**

## Source 3

► Imhotep, Vizier to the Pharaoh Zoser, about 2630 BC. Imhotep may have been Zoser's doctor as well. He is probably the earliest doctor whose name we know. He was later worshipped by the Egyptians as a god of healing.

**Read Sources 1 and 2.**

1 a In what ways do these sources show different ideas about medicine in Ancient Egypt?

b Are you surprised that the Ancient Egyptians followed two different ideas about treating sick people? Explain your answer.

c Which of these sources do you think would be the more useful to a historian studying Ancient Egyptian medicine? Explain your answer.

2 'The Egyptians had little understanding of the importance of keeping clean to avoid illness'. Explain how far you agree with this statement.

3 Do you agree that the Egyptians' greatest contribution to the development of medicine was the medical books they wrote? Explain your answer.

| Egyptian Medicine | | | | | | |
|---|---|---|---|---|---|---|
| **Factors affecting Medicine** | | **Causes of Disease** | | | **New Features** | |
| Factor | Effect | Cause | Evidence | | Feature | Evidence |
| 1 _____ | Efficient farming meant people had spare time and some could specialize in medicine for all or most of their lives. | 1 Supernatural: Spirits or Gods | a) _____ b) _____ | | 1 Doctors | _____ |
| | | 2 Physical causes: | a) _____ b) _____ | | | |
| 2 Religion | _____ | | | | 2 Some knowledge of anatomy – eg heart, lungs, liver. | a) _____ b) _____ |
| 3 _____ | Hindered knowledge of anatomy because bodies could not be dissected because Egyptians believed they needed to preserve body for afterlife. | **Treatments Used** | | | | |
| | | Treatment | Illness | Evidence | | |
| | | 1 Drugs and charms | _____ | *Papyrus Ebers* (Source B) | 3 Physical causes of disease. | _____ |
| | | 2 _____ | Chest diseases | medical papyri | | |
| | | 3 _____ | Swellings and tumours | _____ | | |
| 4 _____ | Understanding of the River Nile helped them think of the body as a series of channels. | 4 _____ | Clearing blockages | _____ | 4 Hygiene | _____ |
| | | 5 Cutting and removing lumps | _____ | _____ | | |

# CHAPTER 3

# MINOAN CRETE

## 3.1 Who were the Minoans?

The Minoan people lived in Crete. Their civilization flourished from about 2000 BC until finally collapsing around 1380 BC. We know about the Minoan civilization because of the work of archaeologists who began excavating Minoan sites in about 1900. Previously the Minoans were known of only through legends and some references in the writings of ancient Greek authors. What the archaeologists found shows us that the Minoans had developed a civilized way of life. They were good sailors and traded widely with other Mediterranean peoples, including the Egyptians.

▼ One of the stone drains at the Minoan palace of Knossos which carried water away from the living quarters.

### Source A

### Minoan hygiene

Excavations at Knossos and other Minoan palaces show that the Minoan people developed an elaborate system of water supply and drainage. Ensuring a water supply in the dry summers of Crete must always have been a problem. In Knossos they built water tanks lined with water-resistant plaster. There were also drains covered with stone slabs to carry away sewage. Rain water was led down shafts to flush away the sewage from lavatories. Other lavatories had holes in the floor where the user or a servant could pour water from a jug to flush away the sewage. Thus the lavatories could be used even in the dry summertime.

### SIR ARTHUR EVANS

The Minoan palace of Knossos was excavated by Sir Arthur Evans. After finding stones which were inscribed with a form of writing, (that has never been fully understood), he was determined to find out whether the legends of King Minos and the Labyrinth had any basis in fact. Using his own money, he bought land in Crete and began a programme of archaeological excavations in 1900. He restored some of the buildings he found, sometimes basing large wall paintings on just a few fragments. He also gave the rooms in the palace names based on what he thought their purpose might have been. Later evidence has not always supported his theories.

The Minoans also installed systems of pipes which may have been used to bring in water from a distance. It is possible that these pipes were carried across valleys by aqueducts, now long vanished. Rain water was collected by stone drains that had tanks to allow the sediment to settle before the water went into the cisterns.

## 3.2 The legacy of the Minoans

Historians are still arguing about the reasons why the Minoan palaces were destroyed. Some blame natural disasters like the volcanic explosion of the nearby island of Thera, that was accompanied by tidal waves and violent earth tremors. Others argue that invading Mycenaean Greeks burnt down the palaces and drove the people from the cities. What is certain is that Knossos and the other palaces were consumed by fire. The ruins remained hidden for over 3000 years.

Thus the problems of water supply and sewage disposal that Minoan engineers had solved had to be tackled afresh by civilizations that followed. It was not until the time of the Romans that the same level of skill is found. Chance events, whether they were natural disasters or invasions of Greeks from the mainland, meant that their knowledge was lost.

**Source B**

▲ The Queen's bathroom and bath in the Queen's apartments at Knossos.

## QUESTIONS

1  What evidence is there that the Minoans had made advances in public health?

2  What part did the Minoans play in the development of medicine through time?

3  How does the destruction of the Minoan civilization show the effect of chance in the history of medicine?

## CHANCE

We usually think of things happening for a reason. In History that reason is often to do with a person or people deciding they want something and then acting in a way that tries to make that thing happen. However many changes come about, or do not come about, because of chance. This means something that is unplanned, but which turns out to have a significant effect. The disappearance of the Minoan civilization is a good example. The Minoans had solved some problems of water supply and drainage which, because of the destruction of Minoan Crete, had to be solved again later. If Minoan Crete had survived this knowledge would have spread through the Greek civilization to Rome. This did not happen because of a deliberate attempt to slow down the development of medicine – it happened by chance.

# CHAPTER 4

# ANCIENT GREECE

## 4.1 Greece 1000 – 300 BC

In the ancient world Greece was an area not a country. The people we call the Greeks lived not only in modern Greece and the Greek islands, but also in cities built on the shores of the Mediterranean, in modern Albania, Turkey, Italy, Spain and Africa. From about 1000 BC the Greeks were beginning to build cities in mainland Greece. By about 750 BC these cities had developed into independent states. Each city ruled over the surrounding countryside. The cities began to colonize by building trading settlements around the shores of the Mediterranean.

The Greeks shared a language and belief in the same gods. The early Greeks explained many of the mysteries of nature by the actions of their gods.

- The changes in the seasons were explained by the myth of Demeter and Persephone. Persephone was Demeter's daughter. For six months of every year she was forced to live in Hades – the world of the dead. This made Demeter so angry that, during this time, she would not allow plants to grow. Every spring, however, Persephone was released from Hades and Demeter, happy again, allowed the plants to grow.

- Volcanoes were caused by Hephaestos, the god of fire. He was a blacksmith and the Greeks believed that the smoke and flames from a volcano were created by Hephaestos while he worked at his forge.

◀ The Greek world, c. 450 BC.

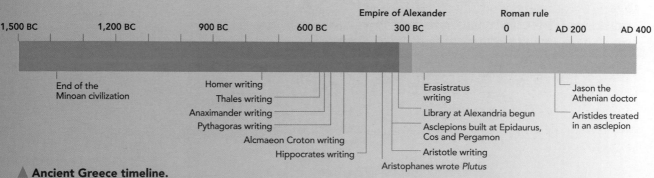

▲ Ancient Greece timeline.

## The Greek world around 450 BC

Greek civilization was at its height between 600 BC and 300 BC. The individual city states developed and became more powerful. While they were all different, they each had a leisured upper class or classes who had plenty of time to spend on their interests. Science, philosophy and mathematics were important to many Greeks. They replaced the old supernatural explanations for events with new **rational** ones produced by thinkers called philosophers. One of these, Thales of Miletus, predicted an eclipse of the sun in 585 BC because he understood some of the motions of the sun, moon and planets. He also thought water was the basis of all life. In about 560 BC Anaximander developed this theory, suggesting all things were made of four elements, earth, fire, air and water. Pythagoras, who died about 500 BC, was fascinated by mathematics. He put forward the idea that life was concerned with the balance between opposites.

▲ A hero from the siege of Troy treats his wounded friend. This painting is from a decorated cup.

## CHANGE AND DEVELOPMENT

A **change** is a completely new idea.

A **development** is when something is based on what went before it – it has *developed* from a previous idea.

Medicine developed too. Our first knowledge of Greek medicine comes from the poems of Homer. Historians believe these poems were written about 750 BC, and based on earlier poems that had been passed down by word of mouth. They tell of the siege of Troy, and of the soldiers who fought in that war. Doctors are described giving common-sense treatment to the wounds suffered by the warriors.

Two different medical traditions developed. One was the rational tradition which we associate with Hippocrates. Hippocrates was born about 460 BC and the medical books associated with him were written from about 430 BC onwards. The other was a supernatural tradition, associated with the cult of the god Asclepios. Asclepios' sons were said to have fought in the siege of Troy and stories about him were common in Homer's time. However the real growth of the cult of Asclepios came much later and the great temples that were the home of the cult were built after 400 BC. It is important to keep these dates in mind. What happened in Greece was not that a more primitive supernatural system of medicine was replaced by a more advanced natural or rational medicine. Both developed and flourished at the same time.

## QUESTIONS

1   Was it possible for the Greeks to have had any contact with Egypt?

2   a   Describe a change in ideas in the Greek period.

    b   Describe a development in ideas in the Greek period.

    c   Was Hippocratic medicine a development from the work of the philosophers?

    d   Was Hippocratic medicine a development from the supernatural medicine of the cult of Asclepios?

Asclepios was the Greek god of healing. The temples built for his worship were used for treating the sick. They were called Asclepions. The cult of Asclepios became more important during the 5th century BC and the three most important Asclepions, in Epidaurus, Pergamum, and Cos, were all built or rebuilt around 350 BC.

As you can see from Source C, the Asclepions were large and complicated sites. People who were ill would go to an Asclepion, spend at least one night there, praying to Asclepios and being treated. When a sick person arrived at an Asclepion they would usually go through the following processes.

- Make an offering or sacrifice to the god.
- Bathe in the sea to cleanse and purify themselves.
- Sleep for at least one night in the *abaton*, a long thin building open to the air on each side.
- While sleeping in the abaton the patients expected to be visited by the god. Some had dreams. Others were probably treated by the priests. The snake was Asclepios' sacred animal; he is usually seen holding a staff with a snake wound round it in Greek carvings. The priests used snakes as part of the treatment in the abaton. Ointments were often rubbed into the part of the body where symptoms occurred. Sometimes the snakes licked the sick part as well.

The patient was supposed to wake up cured the next morning. Sometimes they did. Other times they did not. One of our most important sources about what happened in an Asclepion is an account written by Aristides, a philosopher from Athens, about his treatment in AD 150. Aristides had spent years visiting different Asclepions. We also have the story of a visit in a comic play, *Plutus* by Aristophanes, a Greek playwright, who died in 388 BC.

## Source B

First we had to bathe Plutus in the sea. Then we entered the temple where we placed our offerings to the gods on the altar. There were many sick people present, with many kinds of illnesses. Soon the temple priest put out the light and told us all to go to sleep and not to speak, no matter what noises we heard. The god sat down by Plutus. First he wiped the patient's head, then with a cloth of clean linen he wiped Plutus' eyelids a number of times. Next Panacea [*the god's daughter*] covered his face and head with a scarlet drape. The god whistled and two huge snakes appeared. They crept under the cloth and licked his eyelids. Then Plutus sat up and could see again, but the god, his helpers and the serpents had vanished.

▲ From *Plutus*, a play written by Aristophanes. Plutus had gone to the Asclepion to be cured of blindness.

## Source C

▶ A model of the Asclepion at Epidaurus.

The cult of Asclepios flourished until the end of the Roman period (about AD 400). The practice of taking sick people to a religious site, in the hope they would be cured, lasted even longer. This is what happened in many medieval pilgrimages. Until the middle of the 20th century, in some Greek islands, and in parts of southern Italy and Sicily, sick people spent the night in church hoping to be cured. Cures were regularly reported. This is an example of continuity (an idea or practice that stays the same for a long time). While studying the history of medicine we tend to concentrate on change, but continuity is an important part of the overall picture.

▲ A carving showing Asclepios treating a boy called Archinos, which was made about 350 BC.

## Source E

- Ambrosia of Athens became blind in one eye. She had laughed at being told of cures to the lame and the blind. But she dreamed that Asclepios was standing beside her, saying he would cure her if she would dedicate a silver pig as a memorial to her ignorance. He seemed to cut into her diseased eyeball and pour in medicine. When she woke in the morning she was cured.

- Euhippus had had a spear point fixed in his jaw for six years. As he was sleeping in the temple Asclepios pulled out the spear point and gave it to him. When day came he left, cured and holding the spear point.

- A man had his toe healed by a serpent. While he slept a snake crawled out of the shrine and licked his diseased toe. He woke cured, saying he had dreamed that a beautiful young man had put a drug on his toe.

▲ A small selection from the stone inscriptions set into a wall of the Asclepion at Epidaurus. Such inscriptions, called *Iamata* record cures said to have happened in the temple. Archaeologists have found and translated many such inscriptions.

## QUESTIONS

1 'Asclepions were both popular and successful.'

   What evidence can you find to support this statement?

2 We have a number of sources of evidence about the cult of Asclepios. Study each source in turn and answer the following questions.

   a When it was made?

   b How useful is it (what does it tell us)?

   c How reliable is it (should we believe it)?

The work of two earlier philosophers was important to Hippocrates. Pythagoras (about 580–500 BC) taught that a healthy body was one in perfect balance. Alcmaeon of Croton (about 500 BC), a pupil of Pythagoras, argued that a healthy body had the right balance of hot and cold, wet and dry within it. Any obvious imbalance (a high temperature or shivering) was a sign of ill health. The right treatment would be one which put the body back in balance.

We know very little about Hippocrates himself. He is associated with a collection of medical books, the *Hippocratic Corpus.* We do not know if he wrote any of the books himself, but they were written by his followers. Their importance is in showing us, for the first time, Greek medical thought. It is clear that there was a shift in emphasis at the time from concentrating on the illness to concentrating on the patient. Hippocrates did not want doctors to rely on a theory of the cause of disease that could be applied to every case, nor to depend on religious practices. Instead he wanted doctors to observe each patient and the progress of their illness carefully. He firmly rejected magical causes and cures. This system of observing the patient, which was something the Egyptians had also adopted, was developed into what we now call clinical observation.

Hippocrates emphasized the careful noting of symptoms. This was to help predict what would happen if another patient had the same disease. If there was a pattern in the development of a disease, the doctor would know what would happen next. Hippocrates believed it was important to let illness follow its natural course and provide

## CLINICAL OBSERVATION

Clinical observation is the careful noting of all the symptoms of a disease and of the changes in the patient's condition during the course of an illness. A doctor was supposed to follow four steps.

### Diagnosis
The doctor should study the symptoms of the patient. In what ways is the patient different from normal?

### Prognosis
The doctor should try to predict what course the illness will follow. This should be done by thinking about previous patients with the same symptoms.

### Observation
The doctor should then continue to observe the patients, noting changes in their condition and comparing them to the prognosis.

### Treatment
The doctor should treat the patient, but only when his observations have confirmed his prognosis and he feels confident about the treatment to use from previous experience.

► The tombstone of Jason, an Athenian doctor, who died in the 2nd century AD. Jason is shown examining a patient. To the right (shown much larger than lifesize) is a bronze bleeding cup. It was heated, then placed over a small cut, and then cooled. This created a small vacuum which drew out some blood.

**Source F**

the patient with a clean and calm environment. A doctor could apply natural herbal remedies, but only once he was sure what was going on. But there were times when it was not possible simply to allow an illness to follow its natural course, when doctors had to resort to surgery.

Surgery in Greek times was dangerous. Because dissection was not allowed, doctors had only a vague idea about anatomy. They knew roughly where the internal organs were but had no idea of the way in which the circulation of the blood or the nervous system worked. The surgical Hippocratic books dealt mainly with the sort of procedures that had the highest success rate – the setting of fractures and the resetting of dislocated bones.

# 4.4 The four humours

The Hippocratic books concentrate on observation. There is less material on treatment than on the symptoms of disease and the course a disease was likely to take. There is little about the cause of disease. The Hippocratic books sometimes talk about the body being made up of different elements, and the need for the elements to be in balance in a healthy person. The Greek tradition, however, was to try to work out complete theories about things. A later Greek thinker, Aristotle (384–322 BC), collected these ideas together and produced a clear statement of a theory about the cause and treatment of disease.

He suggested that the body was made up of four liquids or humours – blood, phlegm, yellow bile and black bile. There were also four seasons and these humours were connected to the seasons. Yellow bile was connected with the summer, black bile with the autumn, and so on. This meant it was possible there would be too much of the connected humour in the body in a particular season – too much phlegm in winter for instance. This was a problem because Aristotle believed that, to be healthy, a person needed to keep the humours in perfect balance. Here the careful observations of the Greek doctors must have helped shape the theory. Some illnesses, like colds and bronchial problems are more common in winter than summer. These illnesses are likely to produce lots of phlegm. In the theory of the four humours this imbalance was seen as a *cause* of disease not a *symptom*. Doctors had to treat the patient and restore the balance between the humours. So, a patient who was feverish and hot probably had too much blood in his body. The solution was to 'bleed' the patient – take out blood by cutting into a vein.

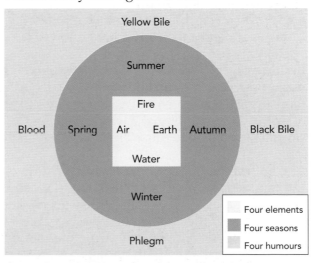

▲ **The four humours.**

Between 334 and 326 BC, Alexander the Great conquered a vast empire which stretched from Greece to Egypt and as far as India. In 332 BC he founded a new capital city, Alexandria, in Egypt. Soon after the great library of Alexandria was built with the intention of collecting all the knowledge of the world. It was stacked with the works of famous doctors, writers and philosophers.

Knowledge of anatomy could only **progress** when human dissection became acceptable. Philosophers like Plato and Aristotle argued that, once the soul of a person had left the body when he or she died, it was acceptable to cut the body up. This meant that people could gain a more accurate idea of the position of organs in the human body. They could examine the veins and arteries, muscles and bones.

Dissection was allowed in Alexandria – for a short time even dissection of the living was carried out. Criminals, who were condemned to die, were dissected and consequently the movement of blood around the veins was discovered. This practice was soon stopped. But dissection of the dead was still carried out, and advances in anatomy were made. The work carried out at Alexandria stressed accurate observation of what was actually there.

Herophilus (about 335–280 BC) worked in Alexandria on the comparative anatomy between men and animals. He also studied the nervous system, and worked out how it connected to the brain. However, he saw the nerves as channels to carry *pneuma* (the life force), not nervous impulses. Erasistratus (about 250 BC) wrote on anatomy and health. He was a very methodical anatomist, noticing the difference between arteries, veins and nerves. He thought, at first, that the nerves carried *pneuma* (like Herophilus), but then rejected this idea when he found that nerves were solid not hollow.

Because of the advances in anatomy, surgeons had a better idea of how the human body functioned, but this did not mean that surgery was much safer. There were still no **anaesthetics** or **antibiotics**, and hygiene was very poor. Unless they had a simple problem, patients were more likely to die than not.

Alexandria was famous for its study of surgery and medicine. Doctors who had studied there went to practise all over the world. But after the first few years, teachers and students split into various groups supporting the theories of the earlier writers. They developed competing theories of medicine and were more concerned with finding evidence to support their favourite theories than with studying what was actually there.

## Source H

Chest trouble is heralded by sweating, a salty bitter matter in the mouth, unaccountable pains in the ribs and shoulder blades, trembling hands and dry coughs. They (the patients) should be treated with a mixture of radishes, cardamons, mustard, purslane and rocket pounded together and mixed with warm water. These will cause an easy and healing vomiting.

▲ From a book written by Diocles, a Greek doctor who lived in the 4th century BC.

## QUESTIONS

1 Was Hippocratic medicine a change or a development? Explain your answer.

2 A doctor who accepted the theory of the four humours might bleed a patient. What would this doctor see as the cause of the problem and in which season of the year would the doctor be happiest doing this treatment?

3 In what way was medical practice in Alexandria a development on Hippocrates' work?

4 Explain how each of the following helped improve medicine at some time during the Greek period.

a religion
b a powerful central government.

## Source I

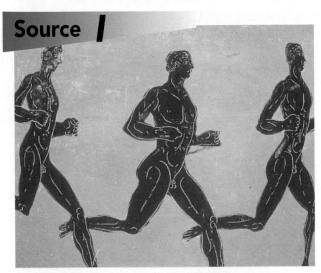

▲ A vase painting from 333 BC showing young men racing. Athletic exercise was thought to help people stay healthy.

## Source J

After waking, a man should not get up at once but should wait until the heaviness of sleep has gone. After rising, he should rub his body with oil. He should then wash his hands, face and eyes with pure water. Thereafter he should, every day, wash his face and eyes with the hands using pure water. He should rub his teeth inside and out with his fingers, using fine peppermint powder to clean the teeth and remove the remains of food. He should oil his nose and ears, preferably with perfumed oil and rub oil into his hair every day, washing and combing it only at intervals.

After such a morning toilet, people who have to work, or choose to work will do so, but people of leisure will first take a walk. Long walks before meals clear out the body, prepare it for receiving food, and give it more power for digesting.

▲ From a book by Diocles, a Greek doctor of the 4th century BC.

Regimen was a word the Greeks used a lot when they discussed people's health. It covered all the aspects of their lives – what they ate or drank, how much they slept, how much exercise they took, what they did as a job. Everything was taken into account. The modern word would probably be 'lifestyle'.

### Healthy habits

The idea of a regimen for a healthy life was not a new one. The Greeks had always believed that eating and drinking well helped to keep people healthy. Exercise and keeping clean had always been an important part of Greek life. The Hippocratic collection of books contained many titles that set out exactly what should be eaten, drunk, or avoided for perfect health, and when meals should be taken. They also outlined the best forms and amount of exercise to take. The advice about hygiene, eating and exercise, if fully followed, would have filled a normal day. Doctors seem to have realized that these were ideal measures which only the rich could take, and gave more general advice for ordinary people who had to work and therefore had restrictions on the time and money they could spend on their regimen.

## Source K

▶ A vase painting, from about 450 BC showing women washing.

Greek doctors practised all over the Mediterranean world. They took with them ideas about the way doctors should behave, about care for the patient, and about prevention of disease. In many places they were welcome. But their welcome seems to have been firmly rooted in the personal experience people had had of Greek doctors. Wandering doctors were as likely to be told to leave a city as asked to stay and practise. But whether individual doctors and surgeons were made welcome or not, there were elements of Greek medicine that had a significant impact on later cultures, both on the kinds of medicine they practised and their ideas about how illness should be treated. Some of these ideas and practices were passed down, lost, then rediscovered.

## A code of conduct

One of the most significant legacies handed down by the Greeks was the idea that doctors should follow a set of rules of behaviour. Hippocrates set out a Hippocratic Oath for doctors that outlined the way they should behave.

## Practice

Clinical observation is used in all hospitals and medical centres today. Doctors always want to see a patient before they prescribe for his or her illness. Records are kept of all the illnesses and treatments a patient has had. When a patient is in hospital, charts are kept to record progress.

### Source L

▲ A Greek painted vase, from about 400 BC, which shows a number of patients visiting a doctor. In the section we can see the doctor is sitting in the centre of the painting. To his right is a man he is about to bleed. There is a large bowl on the floor to catch the blood.

### Source M

The Greeks not only started scientific medicine on its course but also provided the basic elements of our ideas on anatomy, physiology, pathology and our notion of a body having a 'constitution'. It is from Greek that we derive most of our medical vocabulary. Our medical traditions are inherited through a direct and continuous chain from Greek practitioners. It is clear that the debt that medicine owes to the Greeks is great indeed.

▲ From Charles Singer and E.A. Underwood, *A Short History of Medicine*, 1962.

## QUESTIONS

1 a What was the Greek idea of a healthy life?

b In some ways modern ideas about a healthy life are similar to those of the Greeks. Does this mean there has been no progress in our understanding of how to keep healthy since that time? Explain your answer.

2 a Look back through this chapter. Make a list of the features of Greek medicine that are similar to modern medicine and another list of the things that are different.

b Which do you think is more important, the things that are the same or the things that are different? Explain your answer.

# 4.8 Exercise

Study the following sources.

## Source 1

Hermodicius was paralysed in his body. When he slept in the temple the god healed him and ordered him to bring to the temple as large a stone as he could.

▲ One of the Epidaurian *Iamata*.

## Source 2

In an Asclepion the patient was filled with hope and confidence by the religious ceremonies and the stone memorials. Other treatments consisted of diet, drugs, exercise, baths and massage. In addition, at Epidaurus patients could walk over to the theatre and relax by watching plays.

▲ A description of how Asclepions worked. It was written in a book on the history of medicine published in 1954.

1 Read Source 1. How much can we learn about Greek medicine from this source?

2 Read Source 2. Does this source suggest that Asclepions were examples of supernatural or natural medicine? Explain your choice.

3 'The Greeks must have known that Asclepions didn't really work, so they were foolish to carry on using them.' Explain how far you agree with this statement.

4 What part did Hippocrates play in the development of medicine?

5 Was individual brilliance the only factor needed to allow Hippocrates to make his contribution to the development of medicine? Explain your answer.

Copy and complete the summary chart below.

| Ancient Greece | | | | | | |
|---|---|---|---|---|---|---|
| Factors affecting Medicine | | Causes of Disease | | | New Features | |
| Factor | Effect | Cause | Evidence | | Feature | Evidence |
| 1 _____ | a) A settled society – the study of medicine could develop. <br> b) The great library founded at Alexandria. | 1 Supernatural | a) _____ <br> b) _____ <br> c) _____ | | 1 Asclepions (special places for the treatment of the sick). | a) _____ <br> b) _____ <br> c) _____ |
| | | 2 _____ | Aristotle | | | |
| | | **Treatments Used** | | | 2 Trained doctors who examined their patients and had a moral code. | a) _____ <br> b) _____ |
| 2 _____ | a) Stops human dissection in most of the Greek world, but allows it in Alexandria. <br> b) Cult of Asclepios develops centres of medicine. | Treatment | Illness | Evidence | | |
| | | 1 _____ | Any | a) Play by Aristophanes (Source B) <br> b) _____ | 3 Clinical Observation – diagnosis by observation and forecasting. | |
| | | 2 Bleeding | _____ | a) Vase painting (Source L) <br> b) Jason's grave (Source F) <br> c) Hippocratic books | 4 Theory of the four humours. | |
| 3 _____ | New ideas about the natural world encourage doctors to look for new and better explanations in medicine. | 3 Vinegar and herbs, hot sponges, gargles and throat swabs. | Quinsey | _____ | 5 The idea of a regimen for health – a mixture of diet, exercise and hygiene. | |
| | | 4 _____ | Chest trouble | Diocles (Source H) | | |

# CHAPTER 5

# ROMAN MEDICINE

## 5.1 Roman civilization

Rome first conquered the rest of Italy, then most of the Mediterranean world. By 275 BC Rome had conquered the Greek cities in Italy; soon after the cities of mainland Greece fell. Rome was, from the first, a state which wanted to expand. It ruled a growing empire from Rome. Roman rule was efficient and centralized. Decisions were made in Rome, or referred to Rome for approval. Once made, they were carried out by governors of the provinces and civil servants backed by a powerful army. It was vital to keep this army healthy. Like the Greeks and the Egyptians, the Romans were great builders but their work was more practical. Roman building achievements included aqueducts, sewers, roads and bridges rather than temples and monuments to the dead.

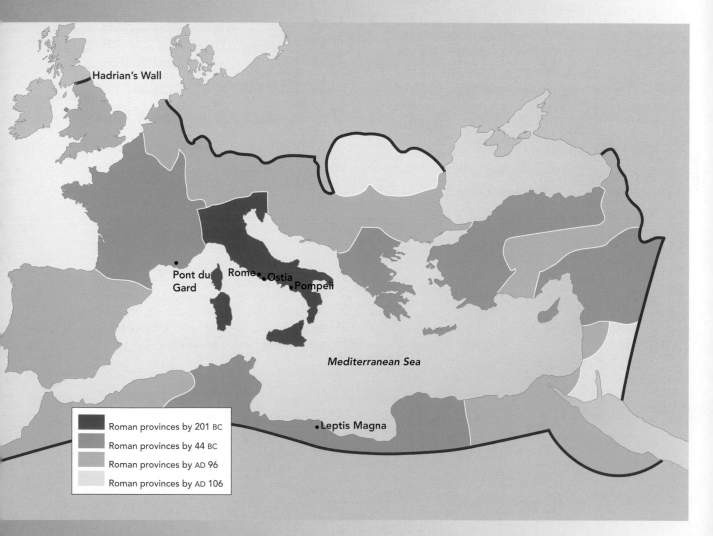

Hadrian's Wall

Pont du Gard

Rome • Ostia

Pompeii

Mediterranean Sea

• Leptis Magna

| | Roman provinces by 201 BC |
| --- | --- |
| | Roman provinces by 44 BC |
| | Roman provinces by AD 96 |
| | Roman provinces by AD 106 |

▲ The Roman Empire.

## 5.2 Medicine in early Rome

In the early years, there were very few doctors in Rome. The head of each household was supposed to treat all the other people in it. The treatments were probably a mixture of common-sense and traditional superstition. Specialized medical knowledge was associated with the Greeks. Since the Romans had conquered Greece, Greeks had a very low social status, so doctors, who tended to be Greeks and were often slaves or ex-slaves, were not well thought of.

During an outbreak of plague in 293 BC the Romans founded an Asclepion in Rome itself, importing a sacred snake from the Asclepion at Epidaurus. Sited on an island in the Tiber, this continued to be a centre for the treatment of the sick throughout the Roman period. It was a public hospital where poor people and slaves could be treated.

The Romans wanted their whole population to be healthy. Apart from anything else, they needed to be able to recruit healthy soldiers. They appointed public doctors in Rome, and throughout the empire. These men were paid by the state, and treated the poor. As the army spread out to garrison the growing empire, hospitals for wounded soldiers (called *valetudinaria*) were

## QUESTIONS

1  List three characteristics of Roman civilization.

2  Are these similar to, or different from, the main characteristics of Greek civilization?

3  The Egyptians and the Greeks both made some doctors into gods and respected all doctors; in Rome this was not usually the case. Does this mean the Romans did not think medicine was very important?

4  Rome had a well-organized government which was efficient at raising taxes. Did this have any effect on Roman medicine?

## Source B

Social and ethnic status of Roman doctors from the 1st to the 3rd century AD

|  | Total | Greek | Greek % |
|---|---|---|---|
| Citizens | 186 | 118 | 63 |
| Freedmen | 170 | 158 | 93 |
| Slaves | 55 | 54 | 98 |
| Foreign, non-citizens | 31 | 23 | 74 |
| Total | 442 | 353 | 80 |

◀ This table lists all the doctors for whom tombstones have been found. Obviously this is only a small fraction of the number of doctors there would have been in those 300 years.

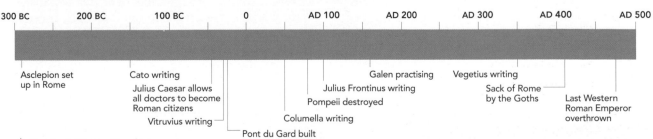

| 300 BC | 200 BC | 100 BC | 0 | AD 100 | AD 200 | AD 300 | AD 400 | AD 500 |

Asclepion set up in Rome

Cato writing

Julius Caesar allows all doctors to become Roman citizens

Vitruvius writing

Pont du Gard built

Columella writing

Pompeii destroyed

Julius Frontinus writing

Galen practising

Vegetius writing

Sack of Rome by the Goths

Last Western Roman Emperor overthrown

▲ Ancient Rome timeline.

set up. Because they were popular, others were set up for the civil servants who governed the empire and, then, still more to treat poor people and slaves who worked on farms.

Doctors were still seen as having low social status. However, in 46 BC Julius Caesar passed a decree allowing them to become Roman citizens, and those who successfully treated the wealthy and powerful could become famous and wealthy themselves. Greeks came to dominate the profession throughout the Roman period.

# 5.3 Public health

For the Romans prevention was better than cure. However, before they could prevent illness they had to decide what caused it. The Romans were a very practical people and they learnt much from observation. One of the things they observed was that people who lived near marshes and swamps tended to get ill, and often die from the disease we now call malaria. Was there a connection between the swamps and the illness? The first solution was to build a temple to Febris the goddess of fever in the largest swamp near Rome. If you believe in supernatural causes and cures for disease, this is the obvious thing to do. However, over time, they must have noticed that there were just as many people dying as before. The next attempt to solve the problem was to drain the swamps. The fewer swamps there were near Rome the less malaria there would be. It worked.

## Empirical observation

This shows two very important things about the Roman system of public health.

- It could only work within the Romans' understanding of the causes of disease. However, sharp observation and common-sense could get them a long way. They realized the swamp was part of the problem, while not knowing the way in which mosquitoes spread malaria. This **empirical** method of solving problems, acting on what they knew was happening rather than waiting until they knew exactly why it was happening, was often used by the Romans.

- The Romans were willing to tackle large engineering projects in order to solve problems. Draining the swamps around Rome cannot have been cheap or easy, but the Romans had the will-power, the resources, and the technology to do it.

Their empirical observations suggested to the Romans that a number of things were likely to cause disease:

- bad smells or 'bad air'
- bad water
- swamps and marshes
- being near sewage
- not keeping clean.

They made sure they took all these things into account when choosing a site for a house, a new town, or a military camp. They also worked hard to get rid of these problems in the great towns and cities they had already built.

## Source C

The new Anio aqueduct is taken from the river which is muddy and discoloured because of the ploughed fields on either side. Because of this a special filter tank was placed at the start of the aqueduct where soil could settle and the water clarify before going along the channel.

▲ Julius Frontinus, the Curator of Rome's water supply, writing about AD 100.

## Source D

There should be no marshes near buildings, for marshes give off poisonous vapours during the hot period of the summer. At this time they give birth to animals with mischief-making stings which fly at us in thick swarms.

▲ Columella, a Roman writer, who lived in the 1st century AD. At one time he had been a soldier but spent most of his life as a farmer and a writer of books on country life.

## Source E

▲ The Pont du Gard aqueduct, which carried water from Uzes to the Roman town at Nîmes in southern France.

## Source F

We must take great care in searching for springs and, in selecting them, keeping in mind the health of the people. If a spring runs free and open, look carefully at the people who live nearby before beginning to pipe the water. If their bodies are strong, their complexions fresh, their legs sound and eyes clear then the water is good. If this water is boiled in a bronze cauldron without any sand or mud left in the bottom of the cauldron, then the water will be excellent.

▲ Vitruvius, a Roman writer and architect who lived in the 1st century BC.

## Source G

▲ A modern artist's reconstruction of a toilet on Hadrian's Wall. Water ran through a channel under the seats to clean the sewage. Clean water ran through the channels in front of the seats.

## Source H

▲ The smaller inner arch is the original outlet of Rome's main sewer, the *Cloaca Maxima*, into the River Tiber. From the water to the top of the arch is over 2 metres.

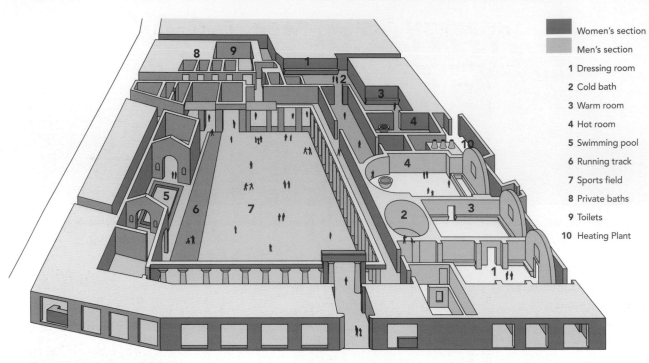

▲ **Stabian Baths at Pompeii.**

| | |
|---|---|
| ■ | Women's section |
| ■ | Men's section |

**1** Dressing room
**2** Cold bath
**3** Warm room
**4** Hot room
**5** Swimming pool
**6** Running track
**7** Sports field
**8** Private baths
**9** Toilets
**10** Heating Plant

## Aqueducts

The Romans used their engineering skills to bring pure water into their towns. There were 14 aqueducts bringing 1350 million litres of fresh water a day into Rome. The water ran through brick and stone channels. The Romans had no system for pumping water, so the whole course of the channel had to run gently downwards. This meant that the channels usually started in the nearest hills or mountains. Valleys could be crossed by building aqueducts, while sometimes tunnels had to be cut through hills. When the water reached the cities it was used for many purposes.

**Source** *I*

◀ **The warm room of the men's section of the Stabian Baths.**

 Emperor 17.1%

Private houses and industry 38.6%

Military barracks 2.9%

Official buildings 24.1%

 Public buildings, baths and theatres 3.9%

 Public cisterns and fountains 13.4%

▲ **The way Rome's water supply was used in AD 100.**

# THE FORUM PUBLIC TOILETS, POMPEII

▲ The area marked **a** on the plan.

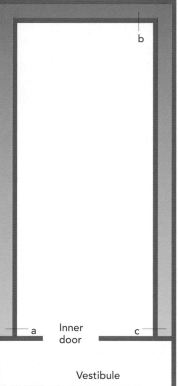

◀ A plan of the Forum public toilet (not to scale).

b

a   Inner door   c

Vestibule

Entrance

▲ The area marked **b** on the plan.

▲ The area marked **c** on the plan.

▲ Looking inside from the vestibule.

▲ The view from the inner door.

Compare the Forum toilets in Pompeii with the reconstruction of the toilet on Hadrian's Wall (Source G, page 33).

What is shown at points **a**, **b** and **c** on the plan?

How was sewage taken out of the toilet?

What are the similarities and differences between this public toilet and modern ones?

▲ The entrance to the men's toilet from the Forum.

## Public toilets

Roman towns also had public lavatories where the sewage was flushed away by running water. There were 150 in Rome itself. Each of these could accommodate many people – there were no private cubicles. Romans could and did meet their friends and sit and chat while using the lavatory.

## Public baths

Taking a bath could be a social occasion too. A visit to the baths could include a warm bath, a hot bath, time in a steam room, a swim, time in the exercise yard or the gymnasium, a massage, resting and chatting to friends, and a cold bath; and all this at a very low cost. Men and women either had separate public baths, or there were different opening times for both sexes if there was only one bath house. The rich often had their own private bath complexes.

We have seen a very positive picture of Roman public health – fresh water, public baths and lavatories, sewers, and state-funded doctors and hospitals. Things were not this good for everyone, however. In the cities, running water was not piped into the apartment houses where the poor lived. They had to collect their water from taps or fountains in the street. The poor did not have lavatories connected to the sewers in their houses either. They used chamber pots and sometimes would tip them out into the street rather than empty them into a sewer.

## QUESTIONS

1 What areas did the Romans try to avoid when siting a town or military camp and why?

2 Copy each of these statements and find evidence to support it from this chapter.

   a The Romans believed that clean water was pure **and** pure water was vital for good health.

   b The Romans thought keeping clean and fit would keep them healthy.

   c The Romans knew sewage was a possible source of disease.

3 How does Source E show the importance the Romans attached to pure water?

4 The Romans did not know about germs, nor that germs can be spread by water. Why, then, did they think pure water was so important?

## 5.4 The army

The need to keep the army healthy, or the population healthy so that healthy soldiers could be recruited, was very important. Rome depended on its armies to conquer and then hold on to its great empire. There were special medical troops to treat the wounded on the battlefield and a number of military hospitals were built. Good water, sewage disposal, and healthy sites were provided for bases whenever possible. Permanent military bases, such as those along Hadrian's Wall, often had bath houses as well. Overall, health standards were very high in the army.

▶ **Vegetius, a Roman military writer of the 4th century AD.**

## Source J

I will give you some ideas about how the army can be kept healthy by the siting of camps, purity of water, temperature, exercise, and medicine. Soldiers must not remain too long near unhealthy marshes. A soldier who must face the cold without proper clothing is not in a state to have good health or to march. He must not drink swamp water. The generals believe daily exercise is better for soldiers than physicians. If soldiers are allowed to stay in one place too long they begin to suffer from the effects of polluted water, and are made miserable by the smell of their own excrement. The air becomes unhealthy and they catch diseases.

# 5.5 Galen

## Galen's life

Galen was born around AD 129 in Pergamum, one of the three great centres of the cult of Asclepios. He first trained as a doctor at the Asclepion there, and later continued his studies in Alexandria. In AD 157 he returned to Pergamum as a doctor to the gladiators. Presumably this work gave him plenty of opportunity to study the inside of the human body – through the wounds. He went to Rome in AD 161 where he soon became famous – both for his success and for his boasting and showmanship. In AD 169 he was appointed doctor to the Emperor's son, Commodus. This gave him a secure place in the Roman hierarchy and allowed him more time to concentrate on writing. He wrote over one hundred medical books.

## Galen as a doctor

Galen returned to the high standards of Hippocrates – especially very close observation of a patient's symptoms. He believed in the theory of the four humours and developed many treatments based on the theory of opposites. Thus if a woman came to him with a cold, he might prescribe pepper. Vigorous exercise or gymnastics would be the best treatment for a man who was weak or recovering from a serious illness. We know about Galen's work as a doctor from his own writings. Unlike Hippocrates, who described both successes and failures, Galen concentrated on his successes – treatments that worked and patients who survived.

## Galen as an anatomist

During his time in Alexandria, Galen had been able to study a human skeleton. However, by his time and for religious reasons, human dissection was no longer allowed in Alexandria. In Rome and Pergamum, Galen could not even study a human skeleton, still less dissect a human body. He knew this was a problem. He encouraged young doctors to go to Alexandria so that they could study skeletons. If this was not possible he recommended that they should always be on the look out for a chance to see human bones. Galen told of his successes such as seeing the bones of a robber by the side of a road through the mountains – presumably the body had been displayed on a gibbet as a warning to others. He also described a time when a flood washed away part of a cemetery, and human bones could be seen when the flood subsided. Galen could not base his study of anatomy on such chances. He dissected animals instead. For many purposes, he recommended barbary apes as the most human-like animal available. For other experiments, however, he felt able to use pigs and other domestic animals (see Source K).

Galen was a close and accurate observer of anatomy through his dissections. However, animal bodies are not like human bodies in all respects. His theory of human anatomy and human physiology (how the body worked as a system) was based on some key errors.

## Source K

Part of Galen's description of an experiment on a pig to show the importance and function of the spinal cord.

The animal which you vivisect should not be old – so that it will be easy for you to cut through the vertebrae.

... Now assume that you have already done what is here described, so that the spinal marrow lies exposed ... If you wish to paralyse all the parts of the body below this section and stop any movement ... then sever the spinal marrow with a cut running completely through so that no parts remain joined together ... If you cut by the thoracic vertebrae then the first thing that happens is that you see the animal's breathing and voice have been damaged. If you cut through between the fifth vertebra of the head, then both arms are paralysed.

▲ From, *On Anatomical Procedures*, written by Galen in the late 2nd century AD.

Galen's study of the brain was undermined by his use of animals. He described a network of small blood vessels on the under-surface of the brain called the *rete mirabile* (the wonderful network). He gave this *rete mirabile* a very important place in his theory of how the body works. Unfortunately it is found only in certain animals and not in humans.

Galen's observation also let him down. He was convinced that there were minute holes in the *septum* which divides the two chambers of the heart. These holes play an important part in Galen's physiology, but there are, in fact, no such holes.

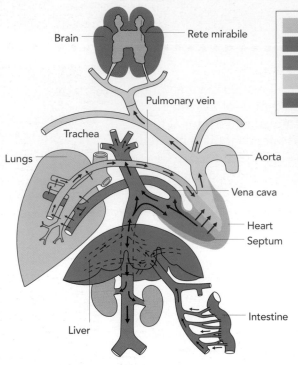

▲ **Galen's physiological system.**

**Pneuma** (life-giving spirit) was breathed in, went from the lungs to the heart and mixed with the blood.

**Chyle** (the goodness from food) went from the intestines to the liver where it was made into blood with Natural Spirit.

**Blood with Natural Spirit** went throughout the body nourishing and enabling growth. From the heart some went to the lungs, and some passed through the septum where it mixed with the pneuma to form blood with Vital Spirit.

**Blood with Vital Spirit** went into the arteries giving power to the body. When this blood reached the brain it was changed into blood with Animal Spirit.

**Blood with Animal Spirit** went through the nerves (which Galen believed were hollow) to give the body sensation and motion.

Diagram labels: Brain, Rete mirabile, Pulmonary vein, Trachea, Lungs, Aorta, Vena cava, Heart, Septum, Intestine, Liver

Legend: pneuma / chyle / blood with natural spirit / blood with vital spirit / blood with animal spirit

## Galen's importance

Galen was the ancient author who had the biggest influence on Arab and Christian doctors of the Middle Ages. There are a number of reasons for this. He drew on the work and ideas of all the great doctors since Hippocrates. He wrote many books, most of which survived. He wrote powerfully, always dealing with possible objections to his theories. In many ways, his writing was like a speech in a debate. Also, he provided a complete theory of medicine; his books dealt with diagnosis and treatment, surgery, anatomy and physiology. Perhaps even more important, although he was writing in the 2nd century AD when the Romans worshipped many gods, his theories were acceptable to Christians and Muslims who worshipped only one god. Galen often talked about *'the creator'* in his writing. He thought of the body as the work of a great architect or designer. This fitted in well with the religious beliefs which were to dominate Europe over the next 1300 years.

# QUESTIONS

1 Galen trained as a doctor in Pergamum and Alexandria. What is the significance of these two cities in the development of medicine in the Ancient World?

2 Galen's first job was as a doctor to gladiators. Why might this have given him some special advantages?

3 Explain, according to Galen's physiology, what happened to:

   a pneuma
   b food
   c blood with natural spirit
   d blood with vital spirit
   e blood with animal spirit.

4 Should historians of medicine see Galen's work as a development or a change?

5 What effect did religious beliefs have on Galen's work?

6 Galen's theory of anatomy and physiology was wrong. Does this mean it is not important in the history of medicine?

## 5.6 Exercise

Study the following sources.

### Source 1

The school of medicine founded by Hippocrates spread all over Greece from the 5th century BC onwards. His methods of observing and recording a patient's symptoms were scientific. The aim was to forecast accurately the course of an illness.

▲ Hugh Lloyd Jones, *The Greek World*, 1965.

### Source 3

When Marcus Agrippa was a government official in charge of the sewers he travelled under Rome in a boat. There are seven tunnels in the city which run into one great sewer. Swollen with the rain water they sweep away all the city's sewage.

▲ From Pliny's *Natural History*, written in Rome about AD 50.

### Source 2

There is no doubt that all these Greek doctors hunt for popularity by using new ideas. They do not hesitate to buy this popularity with our lives. Medicine changes every day and we are swept along by the clever brains of the Greeks.

▲ Pliny criticising Greek doctors working in Rome.

1 Read Source 1. What impression of Greek medicine do we get from this source?

2 Read Source 2. What criticisms is Pliny making of Greek doctors?

3 Read Source 3. 'This source has nothing to do with medicine, it's just Pliny boasting about what good builders the Romans were.' Explain how far you agree with this statement.

4 Re-read Sources 1–3. In view of what is written in Sources 1 and 3, are you surprised to see Pliny making such strong criticisms of Greek doctors?

**Copy and complete the summary chart below.**

| Roman Medicine | | | | | |
|---|---|---|---|---|---|
| **Factors affecting Medicine** | | **Causes of Disease** | | **New Features** | |
| Factor | Effect | Cause | Evidence | Feature | Evidence |
| 1 _____ | Romans could not learn from the drainage and water supply ideas of the Minoans. | 1 Spiritual | a) _____ <br> b) Building a temple to Febris to stop fever in Rome. | 1 Well developed public health system concentrating on preventing disease. | a) Aqueducts (eg Pont du Gard) <br> b) _____ <br> c) _____ <br> d) Sewers (eg Cloaca Maxima in Rome) |
| 2 _____ | Large projects requiring complex organization and a lot of money could be undertaken like public baths and aqueducts. | 2 Bad air, especially bad smells, associated with sewage and swamps. | a) _____ <br> b) _____ <br> c) _____ | | |
| | | 3 Bad water | a) _____ <br> b) _____ | | |
| 3 _____ | Rome's interest in public health was partly because it wanted a healthy army. | 4 Not keeping your body clean and fit. | _____ | 2 New ideas about human anatomy based on studying animals. | _____ |
| 4 _____ | Beliefs did not allow human dissection which held back understanding of anatomy. | **Treatments Used** | | | |
| | | Treatment | Illness | Evidence | |
| | | 1 Pepper | _____ | Galen | |
| | | 2 Vigorous exercise | General weakness recovering from a major illness. | _____ | |

### Source 1

The cult of Asclepios gradually spread throughout Greece until there were more than 200 Asclepions. The cult was carried to Rome in 293 BC by priests from the Greek town of Epidaurus. They had been asked for help by the Romans, who were suffering from an epidemic of the plague. As the Greek ships sailed up the River Tiber to Rome, a sacred serpent sprang from the ship and swam ashore. A temple to Asclepios was built on this spot.

▲ An account of how Asclepions came to Rome. It was written in a book on the history of medicine, published in 1954.

### Source 2

▲ A Roman coin dated 291BC, depicting the arrival of the serpent on an island in the River Tiber.

### Source 3

▲ A Roman carving of the God Asclepios dating from about AD 200.

1  Study Source 1. 'Obviously Asclepions worked or the Romans wouldn't have asked the Greeks to help.' Explain whether you agree with this statement.

2  Study Source 2. Does this source prove that what is said in Source 1 must have happened? Explain your answer.

3  Study Source 3. 'If the Romans were making carvings of Asclepios as late as AD 400, there cannot have been much progress in medicine since Greek times.' Explain whether you agree with this statement.

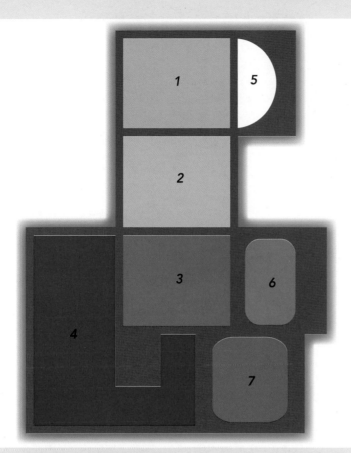

1 Frigidarium (cold room)

2 Tepidarium (warm room)

3 Caldarium (hot room)

4 Praefurnium (furnace room)

5 Cold plunge bath

6 Hot steam bath

7 Hot water tank

▲ **A plan of a Roman bath house**

1 Explain how the Roman public health system worked.

2 Why do you think the Romans placed such importance on having a good health system for their army? You could include the following in your answer and other information of your own.

   ● The fact that the Romans had a large empire.

   ● The importance Romans attached to preventing disease.

   ● What the Romans believed about how disease spread.

3 Who do you think played the more important part in the development of medicine, Hippocrates or Galen? Use your knowledge to explain your answer.

4 When were the greater advances made in medicine, during the Greek period or during the Roman period? Use your knowledge to explain your answer.

5 Which of the following was the most important in helping medicine develop in:

   a the Greek period

   b the Roman period:

   ● the power of governments
   ● the brilliance of individuals
   ● transport and communications
   ● religion.

# CHAPTER 6

# THE FALL OF THE ROMAN EMPIRE IN THE WEST

In the late 4th century AD the Roman Empire was in decline. Tribes of Huns, Goths and Vandals were threatening the Empire. There no longer seemed to be the power and drive within the Roman state to reform itself. In AD 395 the Empire split into two – an Eastern Empire ruled from Byzantium and a Western Empire ruled from Rome. The Western Empire was soon in trouble. In AD 410, the Goths invaded Italy and sacked Rome itself. In AD 476 the last Roman Emperor in the west was deposed by a Germanic chieftain.

By concentrating on Britain, we can see what the fall of the Roman Empire meant to ordinary people, and to medicine. The last Roman troops probably left Britain around AD 410 and the abandoned province was left to the mercy of the invading Saxons. With the breaking of the link with Rome, those features of life in Roman Britain which depended on a strong central government quickly fell into disrepair. Within a hundred years many Roman towns were either abandoned or became Saxon settlements. The water supply stopped working. The sewage system no longer worked. Houses no longer had sophisticated heating systems – a fire in the middle of the floor was more common. There were no more public or private baths. Most significant of all, the strong and stable Roman rule – known as the *Pax Romana* (Roman Peace) – had degenerated into something close to anarchy. In England there were a number of small British kingdoms, all fighting for survival against bands of Saxon invaders.

As a result of this upheaval knowledge was lost. Roman and Greek manuscripts were neglected and destroyed. People with the engineering skill to build, or even repair, the Roman public works died, and no new people were trained up in their place. Within a hundred years, people were living in a country where technology was much less advanced than it had been in their grandparents' time.

## Source A

Well-wrought this wall: Wierds [fates] broke it
The stronghold burst...
Snapped rooftrees, towers fallen, the work of Giants, the stonesmiths, mouldereth.
And the wielders and wrights [workmen]? Earthgrip holds them – gone, long gone, fast in gravesgrasp.

▲ Part of an Anglo-Saxon poem, *The Ruin*, written in AD 700. It describes a ruined Roman city – probably Bath.

## Source B

When you see a dung beetle throwing up earth, catch it and a handful of the earth between your hands. Wave it about vigorously and say:

*'Remedium facio ad ventris dolorum'* [Give relief to a painful stomach].

Then throw the beetle away over your back, take care not to look at it after this. When someone comes to you with a sore stomach, hold the stomach between your hands and they will soon be well. This will work for twelve months after catching the beetle.

▲ A Saxon remedy for stomach ache.

## Source C

Catch a frog when neither moon or sun is shining, cut off the hind legs and wrap them in deerskin. Apply the frog's right leg to the right foot and the left leg to the left foot of the gouty patient and he will certainly be cured.

▲ A cure used by 'Gilbert' a doctor working in the early 11th century.

## Source D

▲ A reconstruction of a Saxon home.

▼ The Dark Ages timeline.

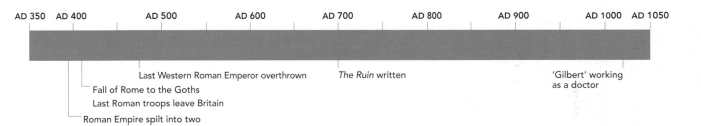

AD 350    AD 400    AD 500    AD 600    AD 700    AD 800    AD 900    AD 1000    AD 1050

Last Western Roman Emperor overthrown

The Ruin written

'Gilbert' working as a doctor

Fall of Rome to the Goths

Last Roman troops leave Britain

Roman Empire spilt into two

# QUESTIONS

1  Who were the 'Giants' in Source A?

2  a  How would you describe the belief about the causes of disease shown in Source B?

   b  How would you describe the belief about the causes of disease shown in Source C?

3  Historians have sometimes called the period between AD 476 and about AD 850, The Dark Ages. Why do you think this is?

4  Did medicine in Britain progress or regress between about AD 400 and AD 800? Support your answer with both reference to sources and other facts about the history of medicine.

# PROGRESS AND REGRESS

In this book we are looking at one aspect of human society, medicine, through time. We need to be careful how we use the technical words which describe the story. **Progress** means something moving forward. In our context getting better, improving. **Regress** means something moving backwards. In our case, getting worse.

# CHAPTER 7

# ISLAMIC MEDICINE

## 7.1 Islamic civilization

The Roman Empire in the West had collapsed by AD 500. The Eastern Empire survived and kept Greek and Roman learning, including medical ideas, alive. Some of these were brought to Arabia by Nestorians, Christians who fled persecution in the Eastern Empire.

### Islam

A new civilization grew up in the Middle East, based on the religious teachings of Muhammad, born in Arabia in AD 570. Muhammad was said to be a prophet, passing on the words of *Allah*, the one God. The followers of Islam, the new religion founded by Muhammad, were called Muslims. The Holy Book of Islam is the *Qur'an*, which describes exactly how every Muslim, rich and poor, men, women and children, should live their lives. Muslims were expected to follow these teachings exactly. Muslims also had to follow the 'wise sayings' of Muhammad collected in the *Hadith*.

### The Islamic Empire

When Muhammad died, in AD 632, Islam was ruled by a series of **caliphs**, who were supposed to carry on Mohammad's teachings. Muslims were told to spread Mohammad's teachings and the caliphs did; sometimes by force. By AD 1000 they ruled a huge empire that stretched from Spain in the west to the River Indus in the east. People in the Islamic Empire all spoke Arabic, and Islam was the most important religion.

The various caliphs were rich and powerful and built beautiful cities, such as Baghdad and Cairo. They grew richer through trade, as they began to control important trade routes. In these cities they set up schools and, later, universities, because learning was important to Muslims. They also built mosques in which to worship. They built public baths, because the *Qur'an* said hygiene was important.

▲ Islamic influence in about AD 1000.

## QUESTIONS

1  How did Greek and Roman learning survive the fall of Rome?

2  What part did chance play in this survival?

3  What is the Qur'an and what does it teach?

4  What united all the people who became part of the Islamic Empire?

All religions influence the way people think, including their ideas about medicine. Religion affects how people behave, and both Christianity and Islam refused to allow dissection of human bodies. This prevented surgeons from studying the human body in order to improve their knowledge and skill. Islam affected medicine in other ways, too.

## The importance of learning

Islam encouraged learning. Books were so important in the Arabic world that by AD 794 Baghdad had its own paper factory. Arabic doctors used the Greek medical texts translated by the Nestorians and collected and translated even more. They took the medical ideas in these books further and wrote their own medical books. So they preserved the medical works of people such as Hippocrates and extended medical knowledge too.

## Treating patients

Both Muslims and Christians thought that diseases could be sent by their God. Christians often encouraged prayer, the repenting of sins and fasting rather than treatment. The Islamic *Hadith* told doctors to try to cure patients: 'Oh servant of Allah, use medicine. Allah has not created pain without a remedy for it'.

## Other ideas

The *Qur'an* insisted on cleanliness. Islamic doctors observed that hygiene was important for health. Charity and caring for others was important in Islam. This meant that hospitals were set up to care for the sick. The hospital set up in Cairo in AD 1283 saw that the patients were given money when they left, so that they did not have to go straight back to work.

**Source A**

▲ Caliph Manum (AD 813–33) having a shower, haircut and massage in the bath-house of his palace in Baghdad.

**Source B**

Keep your house and yards clean. Allah does not like dirt and untidiness. Allah is pleased if you clean your teeth and trim your nails and moustache. Every Muslim must have a bath once a week, when he must wash his head and his whole body.

▲ From the Islamic book the *Hadith*. While the *Qur'an* is said to be the words of Allah, the *Hadith* is Muhammad explaining the words of Allah.

## QUESTIONS

1  How did the teachings of the Qur'an influence Islamic medicine?

2  How was Islamic respect for learning helpful to the development of western medicine?

Arab doctors accepted and used ideas about diagnosis set out in books written by Hippocrates and Galen. They used the idea of keeping the four humours balanced in the body. More importantly, they accepted the Hippocratic idea of clinical observation. They carefully observed and recorded the symptoms of patients and the effects of various treatments, so that they could learn by experience.

### Drugs

Arab doctors used processes that they invented, such as **distillation**, to prepare drugs to treat diseases and to use as an anaesthetic.

### Hospitals

Islamic towns and cities often had several hospitals to care for the sick. Hospitals were also used to train doctors, and a doctor who passed his training was given a licence. He could then set up his own medical practice or work in a hospital. There were still many people in the Islamic world who set themselves up as healers without a licence, but they were not stopped from working.

### Rhazes

An Arab doctor, Rhazes (AD 860–923), was asked to set up a new hospital in Baghdad in about AD 900. He ran the hospital and also wrote about 200 medical books. These were both translations and notes on Greek books and books about his own medical discoveries. The most famous of these was *On Smallpox and Measles*. He was the first to observe and describe the difference between these two diseases. He also wrote a huge encyclopaedia of medicine that covered Greek and Arabic ideas call *El Hawi*.

### Avicenna

Avicenna (AD 980–1037) was another Arab doctor who wrote many medical books. His *Canon of Medicine* was an encyclopaedia of medicine that was translated into Latin, and so brought Greek learning back into western Europe. The *Canon* was used as a standard textbook until about AD 1700.

## Source C

▲ **Doctors in the Islamic Empire used many herbal remedies. This is an illustration from an Arabic translation, made in about AD 1229, of a Greek herbal remedy book by Dioscorides.**

## Source D

All that is written in books is worth much less than the experience of a wise doctor.

▲ **Written by Rhazes in about AD 900.**

## Source E

The main symptoms of smallpox are backache, fever, stinging pains, red cheeks and eyes and difficulty breathing.

Excitement, nausea and unrest are more pronounced in measles than in smallpox, while aching in the back is less.

▲ **From On Smallpox and Measles, written by Rhazes in about AD 900.**

## QUESTIONS

1 What continuity was there between Greek and Islamic medicine?

2 How did Islamic doctors learn their job?

Islamic doctors saw surgery as a last resort, despite the fact that, unlike western surgeons, they had invented a way to anaesthetize the patient. They soaked a sponge in a mixture of narcotics such as hashish and **opium**. They kept a supply of these sponges, dried out. When they needed to use them, they dampened them and either put the whole sponge over the patient's face or inserted two pieces in the nostrils.

## Abulcasis

The greatest Arab surgeon was Abulcasis (AD 936–1013), who wrote a surgical textbook with careful explanations and diagrams. One of the first things he says in his book is that surgeons should never operate before they know exactly what is causing the pain. They should work out what they are going to do and have all their equipment and their anaesthetics ready before they begin, so that they can work as quickly as possible.

## External surgery

Arab surgeons were much more willing to do surgery that did not mean opening up the body. They were skilled in eye operations, successfully removing cataracts and tumours. Abulcasis wrote about sewing up wounds, setting fractures and dealing with dislocations. The illustrations showed doctors how to proceed. Arab dentists were more careful and skilled than western ones. They even made artificial teeth from bone.

## Source F

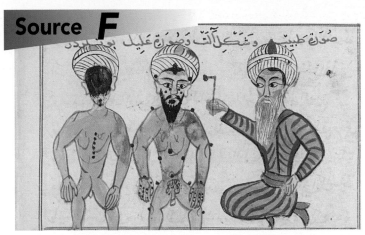

▲ **One of the few surgical practices Arab doctors used regularly was cautery. A hot iron was pressed on a wound to seal it and prevent infection from entering it. In this illustration from a medical book a leper is having his sores cauterized.**

## Source G

I saw an Arab doctor in the hospital who was treating a knight that had a boil on his leg and a woman whose wits were wandering. He applied a poultice to the leg and the boil began to heal. He ordered a fresh diet for the woman. Then a European doctor arrived. He said: 'This man has no idea how to cure people'. He sent for a strong man with an axe, put the leg on a wooden block and told the man with the axe, 'strike a mighty blow and cut cleanly'. The man did as he was told. The marrow spurted out and the patient died at once. He turned to the woman and said, 'the devil has got into her brain'. He shaved her head with a razor, then used the razor to expose her brain, which he then rubbed with salt. She died also.

▲ **Written in about AD 1150 by Usama Ibn Munqidh, who fought in the Crusades against European soldiers in the Middle East.**

## QUESTIONS

1  a  What does Source G suggest about western medicine compared to Islamic medicine?

   b  Why might we need to be careful about believing this source?

   c  How does what you have learned about Islamic medicine support the source?

# CHAPTER 8

# MEDICINE IN THE MIDDLE AGES

## 8.1 Western Europe in the Middle Ages

After the fall of the Roman Empire, Western Europe broke up into many small states. The only thing that unified it was religion. All the rulers would have accepted that they were part of **Christendom**. Only people in the Church, the educated (usually the same people) and some of the upper class would have read or understood Latin. It was for them an international language.

Compared with the 400 years after the fall of the Roman Empire, the Middle Ages were a period of growing peace. Larger countries were developing, like England, and, most of the time, they could maintain the rule of law at home. Little that was Roman had survived. The growing power of **Islam**, particularly in the Middle East slowly became a threat to Christendom and, from 1096 onwards, the **Crusades** brought the two cultures into fierce conflict.

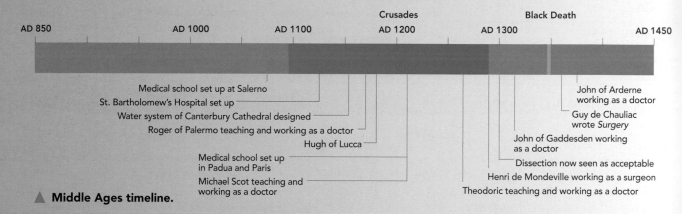

▲ **Middle Ages timeline.**

## 8.2 Beliefs about the causes of disease

Medieval people believed in a variety of different causes of disease. We can group many together and call them magical or supernatural. Others were physical. There were many different people to go to for diagnosis and treatment. There were doctors (usually very expensive), monks from the local monastery, apothecaries (people who sold herbs and drugs) and local wise men and women. There was not a simple link between the type of person you saw and the theory about disease. Doctors could prescribe charms, while many monks diagnosed and treated according to the theory of the four humours, as well as giving simple herbal remedies.

### Source A

I permitted only red things to be about his bed, by which I cured him, without leaving a trace of the smallpox pustules on him.

▲ **From an account written by John of Gaddesden, the royal doctor at Edward II's court, in 1314. He is describing how he had cured Edward's son of smallpox by using *sympathetic* magic.**

## Source B

For scrofula tumours and boils, use the herb scelerata softened and mixed with pig dung into a dough; apply to the scrofula tumours and boils and within a few hours it will waste them and the pus will disappear.

◀ From a 13th century medical manuscript. Scrofula was a disfiguring form of tuberculosis.

## Source C

When scrofula comes to a head cut so that the pus comes out. If they harden and swell for a month or six months, or if the patient is a boy use this oil. At the declining of the moon make eleven poultices of iris and soft radish, use one every day from the tenth day on. Bleed the patient at least once in this period. If all this is not sufficient, surgery must be resorted to. The patient's throat should be firmly held with one hand while the outer skin is cut, then scraped and the scrofula caught with a hook and drawn out.

▲ From the 14th century writings of the doctor, Roger of Salerno.

The Church taught that God could send disease and misfortune as a punishment or as a test of faith, so prayer or a **pilgrimage** to a place like Canterbury, where saints were believed to perform miracle cures, were often thought to be a good idea. This was especially true for people who had diseases that could not be cured in any other way. The planets were also held to be responsible for disease, so medieval doctors were expected to have a good knowledge of **astrology** and **astronomy**. They needed to be able to chart the progress of the planets in the sky. This ability was seen as being just as important in diagnosing illness, as examining a patient, maybe more so.

There were also physical or natural theories about the cause of disease. The theory of the four humours was accepted by most of the better trained doctors. Urine analysis also played an important role in diagnosis. However, seemingly physical treatments, like herbal cures, could often be given for their supposed magical properties (herbs with a bitter taste, for example, were believed to drive away evil spirits), rather than for their actual scientific ones. Many doctors used a *Vademecum* to diagnose illness. This was a book that had the tables of the planets, a urine chart, and a set of rules for bleeding patients.

## Source D

◀ In this illustration from a 13th century manuscript, Edward the Confessor touches a man to cure him from scrofula. Many kings and queens of England were believed to have the power to cure this disease, known as the 'King's Evil', by touch.

## QUESTIONS

1  a  Make a list of the different beliefs about causes of disease in the Middle Ages.

   b  For each belief on your list explain why you think it was an old or a new idea.

2  What theory about the causes of disease lies behind the treatment in:

   a  Source D

   b  Source C?

   Give reasons for your answers.

## 8.3 Growing professionalism

The Middle Ages was a time of change in medicine, though this change was rather slow. The education and training of doctors was one of the first things to change.

Around the late-11th century, the first medical school of the period was set up at Salerno, in southern Italy. There is some evidence that this school produced women doctors as well as men, although it is not clear if these women doctors were supposed just to treat other women, especially during childbirth. The students worked with translations of the works of Galen and Hippocrates, and these translations were later used in other medical schools. Many of the works by Greek and Roman doctors had been saved only because they had been translated into Arabic. These were often translated back into Latin from Arabic. The rediscovery of the works of the ancients, and the discovery of the works of the Arabs was useful in many ways.

- The idea of clinical observation of the patient was stressed.
- The idea that cleanliness affected health gained a wider acceptance.
- The theory of the four humours and balance in the body was also revived.

Less useful was the fact that, for many teachers in the medical schools, what was in the books became 'the truth'. They taught students to believe everything written in the books, sometimes despite clear physical evidence to the contrary.

The medical school at Salerno became so influential and well known that, in 1221, the Holy Roman Emperor Frederick made a law that only doctors who were approved at Salerno could practise medicine. This was an important step forward, although it applied only to the doctors who treated the rich and powerful, and it took many years for the practice of licensing doctors to be adopted by all countries. Gradually other medical schools were started. First Montpelier (12th century), then Bologna, Padua and Paris (13th century). With more schools, the number of trained doctors increased, as did the number of teachers and researchers. By the 14th century, there were many universities in Europe where students could train to become doctors. They were even allowed to witness dissection and take part in debates challenging the ideas of Galen and Hippocrates. It was largely as a result of these debates that some of the ideas that had been accepted for years were revised. New ideas, such as using urine colour as an aid to diagnosis, were developed as a result of close observation of the progress of diseases.

## Source E

When you are asked if a sick person will escape from, or die of, his present illness, look at the **ascendant** [star sign] and where its lord is, since both signify the patient and his condition. Also examine the moon for the patient, because it is a witness of the fortune of this sick man concerning whom the question is made. Afterwards see the tenth house and its lord, since by them are signified health and medicine, or the virtue of the medicines and the advice of the physician. Then look at the sixth house and its lord, by whom the illness is denoted. Then see the eighth and its lord, by whom death for the sick is noted. Then see the fourth house and its lord, by whom the end for each of the aforesaid things is truly indicated.

▲ From the *Liber Introductorius*, written by Michael Scot. Scot was born around 1175 and was one of the most famous teachers and scholars at the medical school in Salerno.

## Slow acceptance of new ideas

Not everyone accepted either the new ideas or the revisions to the old authorities. The ideas of Hippocrates and Galen still formed the basis of the textbooks that student doctors were taught from. Also, while ideas were debated, the debates were not always resolved in favour of the new ideas. They tended to be judged on the debating skills of the debaters, not on the medical evidence provided to support the claims of both sides.

**Source F**

◀ **A urine chart. This one comes from 1506, but they were in use much earlier than this. The use of the colour of urine to diagnose disease was one of the new ideas that became widely accepted.**

# 8.4 Ordinary people

The developments described above were important, but did not have the same impact on everyone. While we know about the doctors who treated rich and powerful people, like popes and kings, we do not know how much these changes in thinking affected the treatment of ordinary people. The medical profession had a group of university-trained doctors at the top, treating the upper classes, who had very little in common with most people who practised medicine.

The changes in ideas had least effect in the countryside miles from the universities, where villagers went on treating diseases in the same way as they had done for centuries. For minor ailments, many people relied on cures passed down in their family that were known to work, or that were suggested by friends. They relied on local people, men and women, who had learned healing as a practical craft and had a reputation for successful magical or herbal cures. These people cared for the sick throughout the Middle Ages, but very few records of them or their activities have survived.

As towns grew, they attracted doctors. Doctors' fees were high. Many people could not afford a doctor when they were sick. Townspeople could ask the local apothecary (who sold herbs and drugs and sometimes charms) to suggest a cure. But they would have to pay for the drugs he suggested, even if the advice was free. Medical care, even at this level, was becoming specialized and beginning to exclude women. There were surgeons, **barber-surgeons** and doctors of physic. Women tended to act specifically as midwives. Some of these people had their skills passed on to them informally; others became apprentices and had a more formal training which ended in joining a guild.

**Source G**

▲ **A woman delivering a baby by _caesarean section_. Women were eased out of medical practice until the only areas in which they were accepted were midwifery and as healers in the countryside.**

## 8.5  Surgery and anatomy

In the Middle Ages surgery was beginning to become a profession. There were two kinds of surgeons: a small number of trained, licensed, well-paid surgeons and a larger number of unqualified 'barber surgeons'. Patients operated on by either were more likely to die than not. Surgeons still had limited anatomical knowledge, so made mistakes. Also, fatal infections of wounds and deaths from the shock of the pain were common.

### Anatomy

Medieval surgeons could have made some progress in understanding the human body, because medical schools were allowed to dissect a limited number of corpses. However, medieval lecturers did not dissect or learn from dissection. As Source I shows, they simply read from the works of Galen, while a 'demonstrator' dissected the body, pointing to the parts the lecturer was describing. Books were scarce and copied out by hand. This meant students could not consult the precious books and each time a book was copied there was a chance that mistakes would be made.

If anyone pointed out that what Galen described was not, in fact, what was inside the human body, they were told that either their perception was wrong or the demonstrator had made a mess of the dissection. Either way, Galen was not to be contradicted.

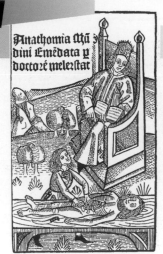

**Source I**

A lecturer reads from a book while his assistant dissects a body. The title page from a 1493 printing of Mondino de Luggi's *Anatomy* written in 1316.

### Minor surgery

Surgeons had most success in external surgery – treating cataracts in the eye or hernias. Some medieval surgeons tried using wine as an antiseptic to prevent infection (Hugh of Lucca and his son Theodoric did this in the late 1200s). Others used drugs to **anaesthetize** patients against the shock and pain (such as John of Arderne in the 1370s). However, these were not widely used.

### War surgery

The Middle Ages was a time when there was a lot of fighting across Europe at various times. In the early Middle Ages, the wounded were looked after by other soldiers, or civilian healers. Later, armies took doctors and surgeons they trusted along with them when they went to war. When Edward I invaded Scotland in 1299 he took a surgeon with five assistants, just for his own use.

Practice made these surgeons more skilled at treating broken or fractured limbs. They learned to remove arrows and cauterize wounds to stop bleeding. Unfortunately, this caused infection, but the pus produced by this infection was seen as a good thing, a sign that healing was taking place.

**Source H**

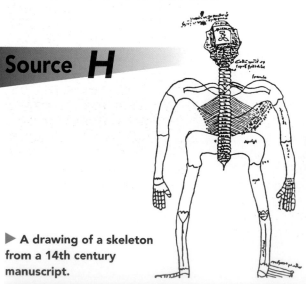

▶ A drawing of a skeleton from a 14th century manuscript.

**Source J**

It is dangerous for a surgeon who is not famous to operate in any way different to that method in common use.

▲ Henri de Mondeville (1260–1320), a master surgeon at the University of Bologna.

## Source K

**To make a drink to make a man sleep while men operate on him:**

Take the gall of a boar, three spoonfuls of the juice of hemlock, three spoonfuls of wild briony, three spoonfuls of lettuce, three spoonfuls of opium poppy, three spoonfuls of henbane and three spoonfuls of vinegar. Mix them together and boil them a little then put into a glass vessel, well stoppered. Add three spoonfuls of the mixture to a bottle of good wine or ale and mix well. The man who is to be operated on should drink the whole bottle by a warm fire, where he will fall asleep and then can be operated on. When you want him to wake wash his face and cheeks with a mixture of salt and vinegar.

▲ A recipe for an anaesthetic from John of Arderne, a well-known English surgeon in 1376.

## QUESTIONS

1 Why were some doctors unwilling to practise surgery?

2 'Galen could not base his anatomy on human dissection. Medieval medical schools were allowed to use human dissection. Therefore medieval anatomy must have been better than Galen's.' Explain why you agree or disagree with this statement.

3 a Why do you think de Mondeville (Source J) gave the advice he did?

  b What effect might this have had on the development of medicine?

4 How did war improve surgery?

5 What might limit the spread of the ideas of surgeons like Hugh of Lucca and John of Arderne?

## 8.6 Public health

The Romans provided piped water, public baths, toilets and sewage systems for their towns. This made it easier for people to follow the advice that most doctors gave about keeping clean. People did not want to live in dirty conditions. But in the Middle Ages, without government provision of any of these facilities, especially running water, cleanliness became one of the privileges of the rich.

### Towns

Ordinary townspeople found it hard to get clean water to cook, brew and wash with. Each town was run by a corporation of rich men from the town. They had to decide how much sanitation to provide and how to raise the money for it. They could not raise sufficient money to provide water and drains for the whole town, nor did they think that it was their business to do so.

People put their rubbish and sewage out on the streets or into a nearby river. Sometimes houses shared a cesspit, or built their privies out over streams that should have washed the sewage away. This simply delayed the problem – the cesspits were a problem when they became full, so were often left to run over.

## Source L

The lane called Ebbegate which runs between the tenements of Master John de Pulteneye and Master Thomas at Wytte used to be a right of way to all men until it was closed up by Thomas at Wytte and William de Hockele who got together and built latrines which stuck out from the walls of the houses. From these latrines human filth falls out onto the heads of passers-by.

▲ Evidence given in a court case heard in London, in 1321.

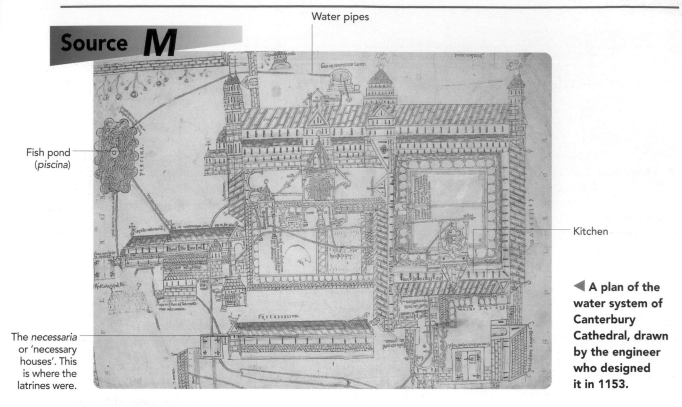

Water pipes

Fish pond (*piscina*)

Kitchen

The *necessaria* or 'necessary houses'. This is where the latrines were.

◀ **A plan of the water system of Canterbury Cathedral, drawn by the engineer who designed it in 1153.**

## Unhealthy streets

The streams often got choked with sewage and became little better than open sewers. Some corporations were aware that it was not healthy to have rubbish and sewage in the streets. They also knew that the river water was not healthy. They passed by-laws to try to stop people throwing rubbish and sewage on to the street – but such orders were hard to enforce. In practice, little was done unless there was a serious outbreak of disease in the town. Then the corporation would clear the streets and collect and burn the rubbish. Town-funded street cleaning was never set up on a regular basis. Concern about public health was sporadic, and only reached a head with the horror of the huge numbers who died in the plague epidemic of 1348 – the Black Death.

## Monasteries

Monasteries were often rich even if, individually, the monks took a vow of poverty. The monks had their own drainage and water-supply systems installed in the monasteries. If their monastery was near a river, they could pipe the water from there. If not, they had to have more complicated systems. The water system of Canterbury Cathedral (also a monastery, see Source M) was very complicated. The water was piped through five settling tanks, to purify it. This water was used to wash, cook and brew beer. Dirty water was drained off and used to clear the toilets. Toilets, in Canterbury and all other monasteries, were housed in a separate building. One of the monks was in charge of making sure that the *laver* (the place where the monks washed their hands and faces regularly before meals and at other times) was clean and always had clean towels. He was also in charge of supplying clean sheets.

All the streets are so badly paved that they get wet at the slightest quantity of water. This happens a lot because of the quantities of cattle carrying water, as well as on account of rain, of which there is a great deal in this country. Then a vast amount of evil smelling mud is formed which seems to last the whole year round.

▲ **Written by a visitor to Winchester in 1286.**

▲ An illustration of a water seller, from the 14th century *Lutterell Psalter.*

## Hospitals

Some hospitals for the sick were set up by the Church, like St. Bartholomew's Hospital in London. Although never as rich as the larger monasteries, they were given money and usually had effective sanitation. There were only a few of them at this time, but those that existed were highly thought of by the public. They provided nursing, clean and quiet conditions, food, warmth, and sometimes surgery and medicine. Not all hospitals had doctors or surgeons – some were only for the care, not the treatment, of the sick. Patients had a reasonable chance of recovery. Some hospitals, like maternity hospitals, or hospitals for lepers specialized in a single branch of medicine.

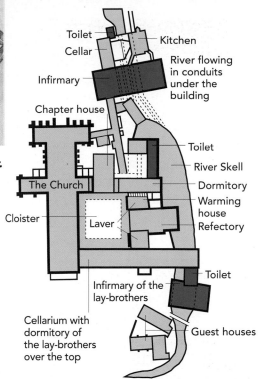

▲ A plan of Fountains Abbey, a monastery in Yorkshire, showing the water supply and drainage.

# 8.7 The Black Death

The Black Death is the name people gave to the **plague**. In 1347–9 the Black Death arrived in Eastern Europe and spread westwards in waves, first arriving in Britain in 1348. People became ill with a temperature, headache and vomiting. This was rapidly followed by the appearance of lumps (buboes) usually in the armpit or groin. The lump then went black and lumps broke out on other parts of the body. After a few days the patient either began to recover or developed black bruises all over the body and died. Symptoms appeared in rapid succession. A patient could be dead within a day.

We now know that there were two main sorts of plague. Pneumonic plague was spread by sneezing. Bubonic plague was spread by flea bites. The plague-carrying fleas came from the black rats that infested towns and travelled from country to country on trading ships. They could live for some time away from a living body, as long as they kept warm. They were carried from place to place either on people, animals or in bales of wool, cloth, bedding or blankets.

## QUESTIONS

1  Water sellers (like the man in Source O) were a common means of getting pure water in towns. Does this show progress or regress in the history of medicine?

2  Describe how the problems of water supply and sanitation were dealt with in

   a  towns

   b  monasteries.

3  Why do you think the provisions for public health in the Middle Ages were so different from those in Roman times?

## Devastating effects

People at the time did not know what caused the plague, how to cure it, or even how to slow down its progress. Despite their best efforts, its effect was devastating. Between a third and a half of the population of Britain died. Sometimes whole villages were wiped out but its effects were even worse in towns. The following sources show various ideas, current at the time, about the causes and cures of the disease.

## Causes

People did not know what caused the plague. They had a variety of explanations, supernatural and natural. They blamed God, the planets, the air. They saw that it was contagious, so avoided plague victims. This was a sensible precaution, even if the reason for it was not understood. Even so, none of the reasons they gave could fully explain the way in which the sickness spread.

## Source P

Many people were unsure about the cause of the great death. In some places they believed that it was the Jews poisoning people. In other places it was the cripples or the nobles. If they found people carrying powders, or if ointments were found on anyone, that person was made to swallow them for fear they might be poisonous.

Whatever people say the truth is that there were two causes, one general, one particular. The general cause was the close position of the three great planets, Saturn, Jupiter and Mars on 24th March 1345, in the 14th degree of Aquarius. Such a coming together of planets is always a sign of wonderful, terrible or violent things to come.

The particular cause of the disease in each person was the state of the body – bad digestion, weakness and blockage, and for this reason the people died.

▲ From *On Surgery*, a book written in 1363 by the French doctor, Guy de Chauliac.

## Source Q

Many wise people think that the Jews are not guilty of poisoning the water with plague, and that some Jews only confessed to doing so because they were tortured. Wise people think the plague was due to the great earthquake which took place in January of last year, 1348. This burst open the crust of the earth and allowed the bad, noxious poisons and vapours to enter the wells and the springs. A large proportion of the Jews are doctors, and they therefore know how to avoid the plague.

▲ From *Chronicron Helveticum*, a history of Switzerland, written by Glig Tshudi in about 1560. He included many contemporary documents.

## Source R

Whoever touched the sick or dead was immediately infected and died. I, waiting for death 'till it come, have put these things in writing.

▲ **John of Clyn, an Irish friar who died from the Black Death in 1349.**

## Source S

The pestilence comes from three things. Sometimes from the ground below, at others from the atmosphere above. Sometimes from both together, as we see a privy next to a chamber, or anything else which corrupts the air. Sometimes it comes from carcasses or the corruption of stagnant water in the ditches.

▲ **Written in 1485 by the Bishop of Aarhus in Denmark.**

## Source T

▲ A doctor attending a plague victim. He is carrying a pomander to ward off bad smells and his assistants are also carrying burners and tapers to clear the bad air.

## QUESTIONS

1 Study sources P to T.

a What medieval ideas about the cause of the plague can be seen in each source? (There is more than one idea in some of the sources.)

b Are these old or new ideas in the history of medicine? If they are old ideas, when was such an idea first held?

2 We now know that all of these theories about the way the plague was spread are wrong. Does this mean these sources are not important in the history of medicine?

3 Which of the above sources are secondary sources for historians studying the Black Death? Give reasons for your answer.

## Cures

People in the Middle Ages did not have effective treatments for the plague. They could not stop it spreading, and they could not save the lives of many who caught it. However, they tried everything they could. They used spiritual and physical cures, depending on what they thought was actually causing the disease.

## Source U

To the Lord Mayor of London. Order to cause the filth lying in the streets and lanes of the city and its suburbs to be removed with all speed to places far distant and to cause the city and suburbs to be cleaned from all odour and to be kept clean so that no further mortality may arise from such smells. They are now so foul with the filth from out of the houses day and night that the air is infected and the city poisoned to the danger of men.

▲ An order sent by Edward III to the Lord Mayor of London, in 1349, the year after the Black Death arrived in Britain.

## Source V

Bleeding and purges, cordials and medicinal powders can be used. The swellings should be softened with figs and cooked onions peeled and mixed with yeast and butter, then opened and treated like ulcers.

▲ From On Surgery, a book written in 1363, by the French doctor Guy de Chauliac.

## Source W

Plague sores are contagious because the humours of the body are infected and the reek of these sores poisons and corrupts the air. So it is best to flee from such infected persons. In times of plague, people should not crowd together, because someone may be infected. All four stinks should be avoided – the stable, stinking fields, ways or streets, carcasses and stinking waters. Let your house be clean and make a clear fire of flaming wood. Fumigate it with herbs – leaves of bay, juniper, oregano, woodworm etc.

▲ Written in 1485 by the Bishop of Aarhus in Denmark.

artikel under cristen gelauben vm

▲ Flagellants whipping themselves. These people thought the Black Death was sent by God because people were sinful. By punishing themselves they hoped God would be more merciful.

Source Y

About Michaelmas 1349, over six hundred men came to London from Flanders. Sometimes at St Paul's, and sometimes at other points in the city, they made two daily public appearances wearing clothes from the thighs to the ankle, but otherwise stripped bare. Each wore a cap with a red cross in front and behind. Each had in his right hand a scourge with three tails. Each tail had a knot and through the middle of it there were sometimes sharp nails fixed. They marched naked in a file one behind the other and whipped themselves with these scourges on their naked and bleeding bodies. Four of them would chant in their native tongues, and four would chant in response. Three times they would all cast themselves on the ground in this sort of procession, stretching out their hands like the arms of the cross. The singing would go on and on and each of them in turn would step over the others and give one stroke with his scourge to the man lying under him. This went on from the first to the last until each of them had observed the ritual.

▲ A description of the flagellants in London by a witness, the chronicler Robert of Avesbury.

## QUESTIONS

1 Study Sources X and Y.

   a In what ways do the two sources support one another?

   b Are there any ways in which the sources contradict one another?

   c Both sources describe a fairly strange happening. Do you think they are reliable?

2 a What ways were suggested for preventing or curing the plague?

   b 'As people in the Middle Ages did not know what caused the plague none of their treatments can have been any good.' Explain why you agree or disagree with this statement.

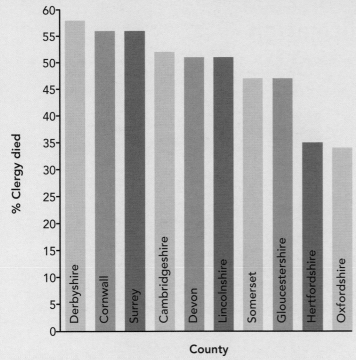

▲ This bar graph shows the percentage of clergy who died in various counties of England during the outbreak of the Black Death in 1348–9.

1 Why did people in the 14th century not know what caused the Black Death?

2 Do you agree that the Black Death spread quickly throughout England because people didn't know what caused it? Explain your answer.

3 Look at the bar graph.

a What use could a historian studying the Black Death in England make of this source?

b 'Since this graph is based on statistics collected at the time, it must provide reliable evidence of the impact of the Black Death.' Explain whether you agree with this statement.

c Do you agree that this graph proves that the Black Death had a devastating impact on 14th-century England? Explain your answer.

Copy and complete the summary chart below.

| Medicine in the Middle Ages | | | | | |
|---|---|---|---|---|---|
| Factors affecting Medicine | | Causes of Disease | | New Features | |
| Factor | Effect | Cause | Evidence | Feature | Evidence |
| 1 _____ | Survival of some Greek and Roman medical books. | 1 Supernatural | a) _____ <br> b) _____ <br> c) _____ | 1 Use of wine as a simple antiseptic. | _____ |
| | | 2 Physical | a) Bad air <br> b) _____ <br> c) _____ | 2 Use of opium as an anaesthetic. | _____ |

| Treatments Used | | | |
|---|---|---|---|
| Treatment | Illness | Evidence |
| 1 Pilgrimage | _____ | shrines and offerings |
| 2 Poultices, bleeding and surgery | _____ | Roger of Salerno (Source C) |
| 3 Sympathetic magic | _____ | John of Gaddesden |
| 4 Royal touch | _____ | C13 Manuscript (Source D) |
| 5 Herbs mixed with pig dung. | _____ | C13 Manuscript (Source B) |
| 6 Cleaning towns to remove rubbish and sewage. | _____ | Order from Edward III to the Lord Mayor of London. (Source U) |
| 7 People punishing themselves so God would forgive sins. | The plague | _____ |

(Factor 2) 2 _____ | Trade with the Arabs meant: <br> a) Works by Galen and other Classical authors returned to the West. <br> b) New ideas from Islamic doctors.

(New Features continued)
3 Formal training for doctors at Medical Schools and Universities. | a) Salerno (11th century) <br> b) Montpellier (12th century) <br> c) _____

4 Books for doctors to carry round with them and use to help in diagnosis. | _____

5 _____ | Urine charts

# CHAPTER 9

# MEDICINE IN EARLY MODERN EUROPE

## 9.1 Renaissance and Reformation

The Middle Ages had been a period of slow change. Between 1430 and 1700 (usually called the Early Modern period by historians) Europe was in a ferment of change. Old ideas were being challenged. New ideas were proclaimed and challenged in their turn.

**Renaissance** means re-birth. It describes the new interest in the culture and science of the Greeks and Romans. Scholars started by going back to the original Greek or Latin texts, many of which were made available for the first time. Scholars not only read the texts but also began to adopt the enquiring attitudes of the classical authors. They accepted the importance of the close observation of nature and the need to make theories which explained the world. A movement which began by looking backwards finished by looking forwards.

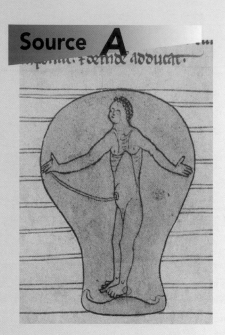

◀ A drawing of a foetus from a medieval book for midwives.

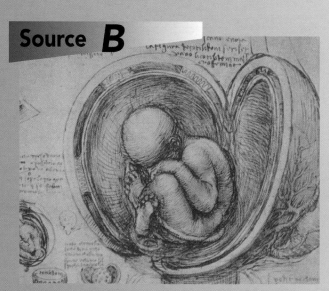

▲ A drawing of a foetus by Leonardo da Vinci. He was able to dissect the body of a woman who died during pregnancy before making the drawing.

There were important developments in art during the Renaissance. The great artists insisted that art had to be based on the most accurate observation possible. Artists attended human dissections so that they understood the structure of the body and were better able to paint it. This, in turn, helped medicine. The artists who worked with anatomists were able to bring a new realism to their work.

The Reformation was an equally dramatic change, this time in religious beliefs and practices. Again it started by looking backwards. People thinking about how the Church should be organized thought the early Church in the years immediately after the death of Christ must be the best blueprint and that later changes should be swept away. The Pope, who was one of the later changes, did not agree.

## Printing

There were important changes in technology as well. Johann Gutenberg introduced printing into Europe in 1454. As you can see from the map, printing spread very quickly. Its effects were enormous. Books were the best way to spread knowledge and ideas. Before Gutenberg, making a book, especially an illustrated one, had been a very labour intensive process. Each picture had to be copied again. Think of the value of illustrations in a book on anatomy. It is not surprising there were very few copies of most books around before printing and that the illustrations in medical books were often poor. A combination of the skill of the artists and the time taken by the copyists meant medical books had been illustrated by drawings such as Source A. Printing and the new skills of the artists meant in future they would look more like Source F on page 63.

This ferment of ideas affected medicine. The changes in attitude happened gradually over half-a-century, but the events of one month, in 1527, sum them all up. Paracelsus was appointed town physician and lecturer to the university in Basel. He nailed an invitation to all people, including barber-surgeons, not just students, to the door of his lecture theatre. Three weeks later he started his first lecture by burning books by Galen and Avicenna. He then lectured in German, the language of the region, not Latin. He went on to say, *'Galen is a liar and a fake. Avicenna is a kitchen master. They are good for nothing. You will not need them. Reading never made a doctor. Patients are the only books. You will follow me.'*

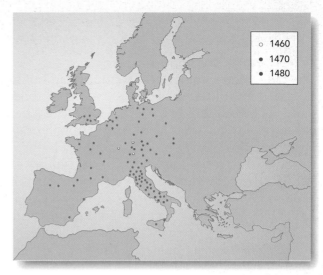

▲ **The spread of printers' workshops 1460–80.**

## QUESTIONS

1  What effect could changes in art have on medicine?

2  'Medicine has often been affected by changes in technology that are not changes in medical technology.' Can this be true? Explain your answer.

3  Within a year of his first lecture, Paracelsus had been forced to flee from Basel at the dead of night in fear of his life. Does this mean his lecture cannot have been important in the development of medicine? Explain your answer.

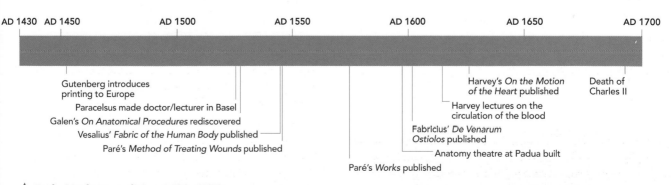

▲ **Early Modern medicine 1430–1700.**

### A new book by Galen

Most of Galen's anatomical writings had not been available during the Middle Ages. The standard textbook on anatomy had been Mondino de Luzzi's *Anatomy*, written in 1316, and based on a translation from Arabic of half of *On the Use of the Parts*, one of Galen's less important anatomical books. Through the rest of the Middle Ages Galen's anatomy was studied through Mondino's version. It was this book that professors read from while dissections were taking place. After 1500 there was a new interest in anatomy. People wanted to get back to the 'pure' works of the classical masters. *On the use of the Parts* was translated into Latin and published in full. In 1531, Johannes Guinter, Professor of Medicine at Paris, published a Latin translation of Galen's *On Anatomical Procedures*, his major work on anatomy – lost in the West since the fall of the Roman Empire. This lost book transformed the study of anatomy. It was vastly superior to Mondino's. Galen insisted the study of anatomy started with the skeleton. He regretted not being able to use human dissection as the basis for his work, insisting it was necessary. His system for the study of anatomy was quite different from Mondino's. It was adopted without reservation throughout the West.

### Vesalius' early life

Andreas Vesalius was born into a medical family. His father was apothecary to the Holy Roman Emperor Charles V and his grandfather, great-grandfather, and great-great-grandfather had all been doctors. Born in Brussels in 1514, he grew up in a house with medical books. He studied at the university in Louvain between 1528 and 1533, when he moved on to Paris. There he began to study medicine and attracted attention as a good anatomist. In 1536 he had to leave because war broke out between the Emperor Charles V and France. He returned to Louvain where he continued to study anatomy. Human dissection had been allowed throughout the Middle Ages, but boiling up bodies to produce skeletons had been forbidden since 1300. While at Louvain, Vesalius went to great lengths to get a skeleton. He went to a gibbet outside the town where executed criminals were displayed. *'I happened upon a dried cadaver. The bones were entirely bare, held together by the ligaments alone. . . . I climbed the stake and pulled off the femur from the hip bone. While tugging at the specimen, the shoulder blades together with the arms and hands also followed... After I had brought the legs and arms home in secret and successive trips (leaving the head behind with the entire trunk of the body), I allowed myself to be shut out of the city in the evening in order to obtain the trunk, which was firmly held by a chain. The next day I transported the bones home piecemeal through another gate of the city.'*

## Source C

As poles to tents, and walls to houses, so are bones to living creatures, for other features naturally take form from them and change with them.

▲ From *On Anatomical Procedures*, **written by Galen in about AD 200 but lost, after the fall of Rome, until 1531.**

## Source D

I would not mind having as many cuts inflicted on me as I have seen him make either on man or other animal [except at the banqueting table].

▲ **Vesalius on Johannes Guinter. He is implying that Guinter did not do any dissecting.**

## Source E

As the gods love me, I, who yield to none in my devotion and reverence to Galen, neither can nor should enjoy any greater pleasure than praising him.

▲ **Vesalius, in answer to criticism that he was unrestrained in his criticisms of Galen.**

## Vesalius at Padua

Vesalius did not stay in Louvain long. He fell out with the professor of medicine over the correct way to bleed patients. He left in 1537 and went to Padua in Italy. Although still a young man, he was appointed professor of surgery. In Padua the professor of surgery was also responsible for teaching anatomy. The next five years in Padua were the most creative of Vesalius' life.

He taught anatomy, breaking with tradition by doing his own dissections, and then by publishing drawings. Many doctors at the time argued that drawings had no place in proper science. Vesalius disagreed. He felt that drawings of various parts of the body would help students watching a dissection, and help them learn about the body before and after dissections. In 1538 he published his *Tabulae Sex*, six large sheets of anatomical drawings. Source F shows one of these sheets. Imagine trying to describe what is shown in words, without the use of pictures or diagrams.

The *Tabulae Sex* showed that Vesalius was starting to see some of the problems in Galen's anatomy, but that he was not yet ready to reject Galen's theories openly. In Source F he shows a five-lobed liver, as described by Galen, but as found in animals not humans. In the first sheet, he shows two more views of the liver. The main one shows the five-lobed liver again, but the smaller view shows a two-lobed liver of the sort found in humans rather than animals.

In 1539 Vesalius published his *Letter on Venesection*. Venesection was the practice of bleeding patients. The medical books of the Middle Ages, following the work of the Arab doctors, said the vein to be opened should be on the opposite side of the body from the site of the illness, and that only a small amount of blood should be taken. This theory was criticized by those doctors who wanted to get back to the 'pure' medicine of Hippocrates and Galen. Hippocrates and Galen had not said bleeding should happen on the opposite side of the body, and had suggested taking more blood. This was the argument which got Vesalius in trouble with the professor in Louvain. Vesalius was on the side of the purists. Other books in this controversy had argued on the basis of what Galen and Hippocrates had actually written, or that certain patients had got better when bled in one way or the other. Vesalius put the argument on a much more scientific basis. He showed, again through illustrations, how the veins were connected. He provided an anatomical reason to accept the theories of Galen and Hippocrates.

▲ One of the plates from the *Tabulae Sex*, Vesalius' first major work on anatomy, published in 1538. This plate was engraved from one of Vesalius' own drawings. It shows the ideas of Galen. The liver (see detail) is shown as a five lobed organ as Galen described it. This is the shape of an animal liver, not a human liver, which has only two lobes.

## The Fabric of the Human Body 1543

Vesalius spent his time in Padua working on his great book, *The Fabric of the Human Body*. It was a comprehensive study of human anatomy, illustrated throughout by the work of first-class artists from the studio of Titian, one of the great painters of the Renaissance. Its publication was one of the great moments in the history of medicine.

- It offered a complete human anatomy based on a comprehensive programme of human dissection. Within each section Vesalius starts from the most complete picture and works down from this. Thus the section on muscles starts with a flayed body displaying all the surface muscle groups, and ends, after each layer of muscles is removed in turn, with a few individual muscles.
- It corrected some errors in Galen's anatomy.
- It offered a method by which the study of anatomy could progress – public dissection and the publication of work backed up with illustrations.
- It broke new ground in the relationship between the illustrations and the text. All Vesalius' illustrations have letters on them. These letters were not just used to key in a list of the names of the parts. Vesalius constantly referred to the letters in his text, making the book one where the pictures and text were integrated into one complete explanation.
- Vesalius painstakingly oversaw the preparation of the wood-block engravings that were used to print the illustrations and every stage in the publication of his work. In 1543 he left Padua to spend months with the printer in Basel so that everything was checked and correct. Because Vesalius' theories were in printed-book form there was no shortage of copies. These were quickly distributed around the great centres of learning in Europe and other anatomists could judge Vesalius' work for themselves, studying the text and illustrations in their own time.

*The Fabric of the Human Body* was not the only book Vesalius published in 1543. At the same time, he produced the *Epitome*. This was a small summary of *The Fabric*. The publication of *The Fabric* and the *Epitome* did not, however, change the study of anatomy overnight. Many of the other anatomists of the day, whose work was challenged and refuted by Vesalius, put up a strong fight. However, Vesalius' method – dissection and illustration – was difficult to argue with.

### Vesalius' later life

Vesalius dedicated *The Fabric* to the Holy Roman Emperor Charles V. He hoped for, and was given, a job at Charles' court. A second edition of *The Fabric*, published in 1555, added a number of new observations, but Vesalius worked on as a doctor not an anatomist. He left the court in 1564, intending to return to Padua and teaching. However, he died before he could return.

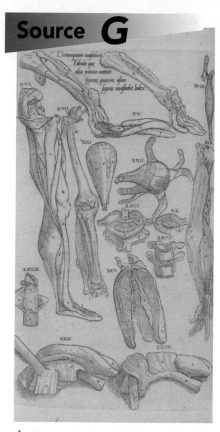

**Source G**

▲ The 16th plate from Vesalius' description of the muscles. Notice the letters and numbers so the parts can be named and keyed into Vesalius' text.

ANDREAE VESALII
BRVXELLENSIS, SCHOLÆ
medicorum Patauinæ profefforis, de
Humani corporis fabrica
Libri feptem.

▲ The title page of the 1543 edition of *The Fabric of the Human Body*. Vesalius is shown doing the dissection, which is taking place outdoors. This was common at the time, and temporary wooden stands were built to enable as many as possible to watch the dissection.

## TRENDS AND TURNING POINTS

A **trend** takes place over a long time. It is a gradual change made up of a series of events.

A **turning point** is something that happens quickly and it may be just one event. Afterwards, things are different in at least one important way.

## QUESTIONS

1 *On the Use of the Parts* was one of Galen's less important books. Why, then, did it become so important in 16th century medicine?

2 Which do you think was the most important book in helping to bring about developments in medicine:

   a  the *Tabulae Sex*
   b  the *Letter of Venesection*
   c  the *Fabric of the Human Body*?
   Explain your answer carefully.

3 Vesalius was a highly talented anatomist, whose books helped to correct longstanding mistaken ideas about how the human body worked. Why, then, did he face so much opposition to his work?

4 'The main reason why Vesalius was successful was because improved drawing techniques made it easier for people to understand anatomy.' Explain how far you agree with this statement.

5 Would you describe the work of Vesalius as a turning point, or part of a trend in the history of medicine? Explain your answer carefully.

## 9.3 Ambroise Paré

Paré, the son of a barber-surgeon, was born in a small village in France in 1510. Barber-surgeons were the lowest of the low in 16th century French medicine. When Paré died, aged 80, however, he had been surgeon to four successive kings of France, and he was the most famous surgeon of his age.

Paré went to Paris to train as a barber-surgeon in 1533. In 1534 he became the surgeon to the *Hôtel-Dieu* which was the only public hospital in Paris. In 1537 he left and joined the French army as a military surgeon, perhaps because he did not have enough money to take the examinations to qualify as a barber-surgeon. He was a very successful military surgeon and, as France was often either at war or engaged in civil war, there was plenty of opportunity to practise his craft. The musket was becoming the most important weapon on the battlefield and Paré developed a new way of treating gunshot wounds. In 1545 he published his first book on the treatment of gunshot wounds, *Method of Treating Wounds*. It was written in French not Latin, the usual language of medical books, as Paré did not speak Latin.

In 1552 Paré was appointed surgeon to Henri II of France and continued to develop new treatments, and to publish books about them. The first edition of his collected works was published in 1575. This led to an attack on him by the Faculty of Physicians, the people at the top of France's medical tree. Étienne Gourmelen, Dean of the Faculty, said Paré was an ignorant charlatan and insisted no medical books could be published without the Faculty's approval. This was the law, but Paré had the king's support. Nothing was done to stop the sale of his works, and they went into three more editions during his lifetime. The attack did spur Paré to write his own life story, *The Apology and Treatise of Ambroise Paré*, which was published in 1585. Because Paré was such a determined author we can study some of his most important cases in his own words.

### Source I

▲ The treatment of gunshot wounds before Paré. This print, from a manual for surgeons, shows the accepted treatment. Gunshot wounds were thought to be poisonous. They were either burnt with a red hot iron (called a *cautery*) or they were filled with boiling oil. People believed this would counteract the poison.

### Source J

Dare you say you will teach me surgery, you who have never come out of your study? ... Surgery is learned by the eye and the hands. I can perform surgical operations which you cannot do, because you have never left your study or the schools. Diseases are not to be cured by eloquence, but by treatment well and truly applied. You, my little master, know nothing else but how to chatter in a chair.

[Later Paré describes the scene after the battle of St Quentin, when the ground was covered with so many dead men and horses and] ...so many blue and green flies rose from them they hid the sun; where they settled there they infested the air and brought the plague with them. My little master I wish you had been there.

▲ From the *Apology and Treatise of Ambroise Paré*, 1585, in which he refers to Gourmelen (my little master) who had criticized and tried to suppress his writings. 'My little master I wish you had been there' is a phrase which runs through the book.

## Source K

Now at that time I was a fresh water soldier, I had not yet seen wounds made by gunpowder at the first dressing. I had read that wounds made with weapons of fire were poisoned, by reason of the powder, and they should be treated by cauterizing them with oil scalding hot, in which should be mingled a little treacle. Before I used this treatment, knowing it would cause the patient great pain, I wanted to know what the other surgeons did. They applied the oil, as hot as was possible, into the wounds. I took courage to do as they did.

Eventually I ran out of oil. I was forced instead to use an ointment made from yolks of eggs, oil of roses, and turpentine. That night I could not sleep, fearing what would happen because the wounds were not cauterized and that I should find those on whom I had not used the burning oil dead or poisoned. This made me rise up very early to visit them. To my surprise I found those to whom I gave my ointment feeling little pain, and their wounds without inflammation or swelling, having rested reasonably well during the night. Whereas the others, on whom I used the boiling oil, were feverish, with great pain and swelling about the edges of their wounds. And then I resolved with myself never so cruelly to burn poor men wounded with gunshot.

▲ An account of his discovery of his improved method for treating gunshot wounds, from *The Apology*, 1585. Paré had published an account of this method of treatment as early as 1545.

## Source L

### Where the amputation must be made

Let us suppose that the foot is mortified, even to the ankle. You must carefully mark in what place you must cut it off. You shall cut off as little that is sound as you possibly can.

### How the amputation must be performed

The first care must be of the patient's strength. Let him be nourished with meats, yolks of eggs, and bread toasted and dipped in wine. Then let him be placed as is fit, and draw the muscles upwards toward the sound parts, and let them be tied with a ligature a little above the place which is to be cut. This ligature has three uses. First to hold the muscles and skin drawn up so that later they may cover the ends of the cut bones. Second to slow the flow of blood by pressing and shutting up the veins and arteries. Third it must dull the sense of the part. When you have made your ligature cut the flesh even to the bone with a sharp and well-cutting knife or with a crooked knife.

If you leave anything but bone to be cut by the saw you will put the patient to excessive pain. When you come to the bared bone cut it with a little saw, some foot and three inches long. Then you must smooth the front of the bone that the saw has made rough.

### How to stop the bleeding

Let it bleed a little then let the veins and arteries be tied up as speedily as you can so that the course of the flowing blood may be stopped. This may be done by taking hold of the vessels with your Crow's Beak, which looks like this.

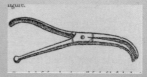

The ends of the vessels lying hidden in the flesh, must be drawn out with this instrument. When you have so drawn them forth bind them with double thread.

Formerly I used to stop the bleeding in another way, of which I am ashamed, but what should I do. I had observed my masters whose method I intended to follow, who used hot irons. This kind of treatment could not but bring great and tormenting pain to the patient. And truly of those that were burnt, the third part scarce recovered. I entreat all surgeons to leave this old and too cruel way of healing, and embrace this new.

▲ From *Of Amputations*, which appeared in Paré's *Works*, 1575.

Some years ago a certain gentleman who had a bezoar stone bragged before King Charles, of the most certain effect of this stone against all manner of poisons. Then the king asked of me, whether there was any antidote which worked against all poisons. I answered that nature could not allow it, for neither do all poisons have the same effects, not do they arise from one cause. Thus each must be withstood by its proper and contrary antidote, as to the hot, that which is cold. And that it was an easy matter to test this on someone condemned to be hanged.

The idea pleased the king. There was a cook brought in who was to have been hanged for stealing two silver dishes out of his master's house. The king desired first to know whether he would take the poison on this condition, that if the antidote, which was said to work against all poisons and which would be given to him straight after the poison, worked he should go free. The cook answered cheerfully that he was willing to undergo the hazard.

Therefore he had poison given to him by the apothecary, and presently after the poison some of the bezoar. After a while he began to vomit and move his bowels with grievous torments, and to cry out that his inward parts were burnt with fire. Because of this he was thirsty and asked for water which was given to him.

After an hour I went to him. I found him on the ground like a beast on his hands and feet, with his tongue thrust forth out of his mouth, his eyes fiery, vomiting, with cold sweats, and blood flowing from his ears, nose, mouth, anus and penis. I gave him eight ounces [227 grams] of oil to drink, but it did him no good for it was too late. At length he died in great torment seven hours after he took the poison. I opened his body and found the bottom of his stomach black and dry as if it had been burnt. From this I understood that he had been given sublimate, which the bezoar could not overcome. Wherefore the king commanded to burn it.

▲ From *Of Bezoar* which appeared in Paré's *Works*, 1575.

### The importance of Paré

Paré understood how to test a theory to see whether it was worth following or not. This is at the heart of modern scientific thinking, and it was a very important development in the 16th century. Paré's story of the cook seems very brutal, but he proved the idea that the **bezoar stone** was an antidote for all poisons was false. Many more lives could have been lost if the theory that bezoar stone was a universal antidote had just been accepted. Doctors would have found explanations for why it didn't work, and carried on using it. In fact they did carry on using it in all sorts of treatments. Paré was also careful to make all his ideas public knowledge. He wanted other doctors to accept them and start using them (and of course accept he was a great doctor and surgeon). In order to progress medicine needs this free flow of ideas.

## QUESTIONS

1  a  Describe the treatment for gunshot wounds before Paré.

   b  Describe Paré's treatment for gunshot wounds.

   c  What was the role of chance in Paré's treatment?

   d  Was chance the only factor involved in this new treatment?

   e  'Chance has only helped medicine to progress, it has never held it back.' Is this statement true? Support your answer with reasons and at least one example.

2  a  Describe the way in which doctors before Paré had stopped bleeding after an amputation.

   b  Describe Paré's new method of stopping bleeding after amputation.

   c  Paré said he had got the idea of ligatures from Galen's writing about the best way to stop wounds bleeding. Why might he have mentioned Galen?

3  What is important about Paré's test of the bezoar stone?

4  You have mainly studied Paré's work from his own writings. Are there any dangers or advantages in this?

## Believing and seeing

Sometimes knowing what you are looking at helps you to see it. The drawing on the right illustrates this point. Is it a vase, or is it silhouettes of two people facing each other? You can see it both ways. This is because seeing, for us, is not just the same as a camera taking a picture. Our brains interpret what we see and fit it in with our understanding of the world. This is one of the reasons why anatomists working on the human body did not instantly solve all the problems of how the body worked. They understood the body through Galen's system, so they tended to see things Galen's system made them expect to see.

Another important part of our ability to understand things is our ability to use ideas we already have. We think of something as being *like* something else. In the previous paragraph *seeing* is described as not being like a camera. Because we all know roughly what a camera does this makes sense. An *eye* might be like a camera, *seeing* isn't. Obviously before cameras were invented this example would not have been possible. All anatomists have used examples like this. Galen's included fire, and what happens in brewing and metal smelting. Just before Harvey was born pumps were developed which were used to pump water out of mines, or to pump water onto fires for fire fighting. Because of this Harvey had a possible comparison to help him explain what the heart does, that had not been available to Galen.

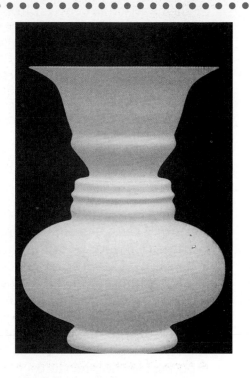

## Vesalius changes his mind

In *The Fabric of the Human Body*, published in 1543, Vesalius accepted Galen's theory that blood passed from one side of the heart to the other through the septum (see page 38). He admitted the holes were so small they couldn't be seen, but still accepted they were there. In the second edition of *The Fabric*, in 1555, he went one step further and said that as there were no holes, blood could not pass from one side of the heart to the other. Vesalius' successor at Padua, Realdo Colombo, showed that the blood passed from one side of the heart to the other via the lungs in *De Re Anatomica* published in 1559. A later professor of anatomy at Padua, Geronimo Fabricius, identified the valves in the veins (*De Venarum Ostiolis*, 1603). Fabricius taught William Harvey, and also designed the new anatomy theatre at Padua.

Source **N**

▶ **The anatomy theatre at Padua, built in 1594. Before this theatre was built, human dissection was usually carried out in the open air, with temporary stands erected so as many people as possible could see. Source H (page 65) shows a typical scene. Fabricius' theatre enabled everyone in the audience to have a close view of what was going on.**

## Harvey's early life

William Harvey was born in 1578 and studied medicine at Padua between 1598 and 1602. Fabricius taught him anatomy. After leaving Padua he worked in London first as a doctor and later as lecturer in anatomy at the Royal College of Surgeons. From 1618 he was also physician to James I and then Charles I.

## Harvey's theory

Most great scientists are great designers of experiments that will give them evidence to test or prove their theory. Harvey had many problems which needed careful testing. His first problem was that he wanted to study the body as a living system. Dead bodies do not have a heartbeat. He worked out when it was acceptable to base his conclusions on animals and when he had to use humans. He did comparative studies on the hearts of humans and animals, and came to the conclusion he could study the way the heart worked in animals. The advantage of this was he could do experiments on live animals, exposing their hearts so he could study them while they were still alive. Unfortunately the hearts of the first animals he worked on beat so fast he couldn't see what was happening. He solved this problem by working on cold-blooded animals like frogs – their hearts beat much more slowly so he could see each separate expansion and contraction.

Harvey's study of beating hearts showed him that the heart was pushing out large volumes of blood. This blood was expelled, or pumped, when the heart contracted, which happened at the same time as the pulse which could be felt in the neck and at the wrist. He next tried to calculate how much blood the heart was pumping out. He realized so much blood was being pumped that it could not, as Galen thought, be being used up and replaced by new blood all the time. This suggested that there was a fixed volume of blood in the body. It was **circulating**. Harvey still needed to explain how this worked before his theory could be said to make sense. He turned his attention to the flaps or valves in the veins that his old teacher Fabricius had discovered. Harvey devised an experiment which showed that the valves allowed blood to flow only one way. Now the theory fitted together. Blood flowed out from the heart through the arteries. It flowed back through the veins, and the valves in the veins made sure blood could only flow back to the heart through them.

Harvey's theory replaced Galen's, which was itself a refinement of earlier Greek theories. Harvey showed that blood was not continually being made and used. There was a fixed volume of blood in the body. By implication his theory also meant the practice of bleeding did not make sense. It was unlikely there could be too much blood, since it was circulating not being made all the time. Harvey announced his theory in 1616, but first published it in *On the Motion of the Heart*, in 1628.

# Source O

These two movements, one of the auricles and the other of the ventricles, occur successively but so harmoniously and rhythmically that both (appear to) happen together and only one movement can be seen, especially in warmer animals in rapid movement. This is comparable with what happens in machines in which, with one wheel moving another, all seem to be moving at once. It also recalls that mechanical device fitted to firearms in which, on pressure to a trigger, a flint falls and strikes and advances the steel, a spark is evoked and falls upon the powder, the powder is fired and the flame leaps inside and spreads, and the ball flies out and enters the target; all these movements, because of their rapidity, seeming to happen at once as in the wink of an eye.

▲ From *An Anatomical Treatise on the Motion of the Heart*, written by William Harvey in 1628.

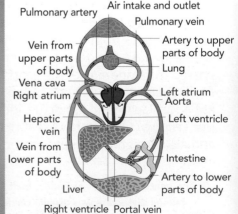

▲ Harvey's physiological system.

## Source P

The pump is easy to understand: there are two valves within it, one below to open when the handle is lifted up and to shut when it is down, and another to open to let out the water; and at the end of the said machine there is a man who holds the copper pipe, turning it from side to side to the place where the fire shall be.

▲ Salomon de Caus describing a machine for putting out fires in his book, *Les Raisons de Forces Mouvantes*, 1615.

## Source Q

▲ An illustration from Fabricius' *De venarum ostiolis*, 1603, showing the nodes or valves in the veins.

## Source R

▲ A print showing a pump for putting out fires, from a book published in 1673.

## Source S

▲ An illustration from Harvey's *An Anatomical Treatise on the Motion of the Heart*, 1628, A simple experiment to show how valves in the veins allow blood to flow in one direction but not the other.

## QUESTIONS

1　What is the significance of the following in the study of the heart and blood:

  a　Vesalius' changed view of the septum
  b　Colombo's work
  c　Fabricius' work?

2　Explain the importance of the following steps in Harvey's theory:

  a　the use of animals
  b　the use of frogs in particular
  c　the volume of blood the heart pumps
  d　the valves in the veins?

3　a　How did a 17th century fire pump work?
  b　In what way is this similar to the heart?
  c　How does Harvey use examples in Source O?

4　Was Harvey's work a development or a change in the history of medicine?

5　Galen's idea that blood moved through the septum was wrong. Does this mean his views about the heart are not important in the history of medicine?

6　Harvey announced his theory of the circulation of blood in 1616 while he was still working as a doctor. Would you expect him to have gained or lost patients after this?

## 9.5 Treatment

The Early Modern period saw important advances in medicine. The work of Vesalius and Harvey, in particular, meant great progress was made in anatomy. However, while there was a move to a more scientific approach in many areas of medicine, there was still widespread belief in magical causes and cures, especially in treating diseases.

Townspeople had more kinds of treatment available to them than people who lived in the countryside. Trained, licensed, doctors were the most expensive. Apothecaries, people who mixed medicines, often suggested treatments, as chemists do today. Below these two groups were people with varying experience and skill who claimed to be healers.

## The first choice of treatment

Letters and diaries from the time show that the sick often tried a variety of treatments. Many began by treating themselves, the cheapest, easiest route. Household recipe books that have survived from the time often include medicines such as 'a syrup for the head ache' or 'a salve for wounds'. These were usually simple herbal remedies. If self-treatment failed, people needed outside help.

## Trained doctors

From 1600 the Royal College of Physicians trained and licensed university-educated doctors who practiced mainly in the towns and cities. There were about 50 of these doctors in London in the early 1600s. They wanted to stop other people working as healers and claimed that untrained healers were dangerous. In fact, patients were usually better off with an experienced healer than a doctor. A licence did not guarantee the best treatment, just the most expensive one.

## Apothecaries

Apothecaries mixed medicines and were mainly based in towns and cities. They used herbs, fruits, vegetables and spices. These they boiled, dried, pressed and distilled to make pills, syrups ointments (mixed with fat) and poultices to place on wounds.

As well as herbal cures, apothecaries mixed chemical, even toxic cures. These they usually made up for practitioners who believed in the medical ideas of Paracelsus, who had stated that rather than humours the body had a chemical makeup and should be treated with chemicals. These chemicals included mercury, sulphur, lead, gold, pearls (dissolved in vinegar) and even nitric acid.

As well as mixing medicines to fit the prescriptions given out by doctors, many apothecaries gave medical advice and sold medicines to patients directly.

## Source T

▲ *The Doctor's Shop*, painted in Holland in the 1660s. The painting was intended to show the range of medicines a doctor or apothecary could provide.

## Other healers

After licensed doctors and apothecaries, the sick could turn to any number of different kinds of people who called themselves healers. There were far more 'amateur' healers than licensed doctors and apothecaries. There was about one healer for every 400 people in rural areas in about 1600, and one for every 250 in the towns.

Local gentry often treated the poor in their area, usually with herbal medicines. In villages especially there was likely to be someone who was known to give good medical advice or treatment.

## Cures

The cures used by local healers could range from practising common sense and prescribing herbal cures to relying on supernatural cures. The supernatural cures, and healers, varied wildly. Some of the more respectable healers simply suggested praying to God would be the most effective cure. Other healers claimed to be witches. They had a range of cures from magical spells to ointments and potions that were made under 'magical' conditions – with herbs picked during a full moon while chanting spells, for example. There were also faith healers, who believed that their faith gave them the power to heal the sick.

## Women

Women lost some of their status in the Early Modern period, due to the opposition of licensed doctors to women practicing medicine. However, in rural areas they probably still made up the largest number of healers. Even in the towns, women kept their traditional role as midwives. In some towns, town councils were established and these undertook to provide for the sick poor, employing poor women to act as nurses. These women also looked after people who were isolated in 'lazarhouses' because they had infectious diseases.

▲ This engraving, made in 1580, shows a woman giving birth. She is being helped by a midwife and comforted by her friends. The doctors in the background are working out the baby's horoscope. For those who believed that the planets affected health and everyday life, this was an important job.

Unlicensed doctors are but charlatans. Women, especially, should not practice medicine because they do not have the natural authority of men. Also, they do not have enough understanding or a large enough capacity for reasoning. In this way, they might misdiagnose the disease and kill the patient.

▲ John Cotta, a licensed doctor practising in Northamptonshire from about 1570, wrote this in a book about unlicensed healers in 1612. He followed this book with two more about how to recognize and counteract witchcraft.

### New treatments

Many licensed and unlicensed healers used the same treatments and approaches to disease. At the beginning of the Early Modern period almost all healers worked to keep the patient 'in balance', according to the four humours theory (see page 25). Some, but not all of them, tied this balance to the movements of the stars and planets.

### A new outlook

As the Early Modern period progressed people became more open in their attitudes to disease. It was a time where people stressed the importance of observation and experimentation, rather than relying on book learning.

### Trying everything

In the spirit of investigation, the end of the Early Modern period saw more magical practices in use than at the beginning of the period. For example, King Charles II re-introduced touching people to cure scrofula. The idea that the king's touch could cure this disease was prevalent in the Middle Ages (see page 49 Source D) but lapsed in Tudor times. Similarly, while there had been a tendency for the most important people to use licensed doctors, Charles II sent for the Irish faith healer, Valentine Greatrakes so that he could see him perform his miracles.

Charles II did not send for the Valentine Greatrakes when he was sick. He sent for his personal doctor, Thomas Sydenham. Sydenham was a great believer in the close observation of patients and their symptoms. He advised a young man who wanted to be a doctor, 'Anatomy, botany – nonsense. Sir, I know an old woman in the flower market who understands botany better. As for anatomy, my butcher can dissect a joint just as well. No, young man. You must go to the bedside. It is there alone you can learn about disease.'

## THE ROYAL SOCIETY

The Royal Society was set up in 1662. It was part of the new move to experiment, and King Charles himself was its patron. Samuel Pepys, the famous diarist, was a member and went to many meetings. The Royal Society investigated whatever the members were interested in, including medical and scientific ideas. Pepys went to experiments on:

- the effect of heat on glass
- a newly invented musical instrument
- the baking of French bread
- comets
- the effect of poison on dogs, cats and hens
- the effect of a vacuum on a kitten
- the design of coaches
- the human foetus
- the process of feltmaking
- blood transfusions and circulation
- the refraction of light
- microscopes
- the qualities of gunpowder.

## QUESTIONS

1 a  In what ways might growing professionalism have been a good thing for medical practice?

  b  In what ways might it have been bad thing?

2 a  How might new ideas about experiments be seen to have pushed medical progress backwards?

  b  How might the changed outlook be good for medical practice?

## Source 1

▲ A painting from 1556 by Pieter Bruegel. The purpose of the picture was to make fun of barber-surgeons. The painting is called *Cutting out the Stone of Madness*.

## Source 2

Paré's use of ligatures was not totally new, but it had never become popular because many surgeons believed that using it was taking too much of a risk. He was prepared to try new ideas even if it meant going against the methods that other surgeons had followed for centuries.

In one way Paré's critics were right, although they did not understand why. Paré's ligatures did stop the bleeding, but they were dangerous because the threads themselves could carry infection into the wound.

## Source 3

Although Paré did not know much about germs or anaesthetics, he certainly made improvements in surgery. However, many of his improvements were ignored and surgeons continued to use the cautery iron and work in filthy conditions. As one historian has said 'After Paré's time, infection in surgery was more common. The full benefit of using ligatures was not seen until Lister showed how surgical infection was spread.

◀▲ Extracts from a recent book on the history of medicine, commenting on Paré's work.

**Copy and complete the summary chart below.**

| Early Modern Medicine | | | | | | |
|---|---|---|---|---|---|---|
| **Factors affecting Medicine** | | **Causes of Disease** | | | **New Features** | |
| Factor | Effect | Cause | Evidence | | Feature | Evidence |
| **1** Communications: a) development of printing b) accuracy of drawing | _____ | Physical causes: The Four Humours, Supernatural causes | _____ | | Improvements in anatomy: **1** Vesalius ensures anatomy based on human dissection, corrects many errors, and establishes need for illustration in anatomical books. | _____ |
| | | **Treatments Used** | | | | |
| | | Treatment | Illness | Evidence | | |
| **2** Technology: the invention of pumps to drain mines and fight fires. | _____ | **1** Cautery | Gunshot wounds and amputations | _____ | **2** Function of the heart and circulation of the blood discovered. | _____ |
| **3** _____ | Wounds treated led to new treatments being developed such as Paré's use of ligatures. | **2** Ointment and bandaging | Gunshot wounds | | Improvements in surgery: use of ligatures in amputations. | _____ |
| | | **3** Ligature, and tying blood vessels with thread. | Amputations | _____ | A more scientific attitude to proof – especially the growing use of experiments. | a) Vesalius' use of public dissection to prove his theories. b) _____ c) Harvey's experiments described in *On the Motion of the Heart*, 1628. |
| | | **4** _____ | Any illness | Robert Burton | | |
| **4** _____ | Paré developed his new treatment for gunshot wounds because he ran out of boiling oil to use as a cautery. | **5** Bleeding and purging | Illnesses with fever, swelling and/or convulsions | | Printed books made new ideas more widely available more quickly. | _____ |

**1** Look at Source 1.

**a** What evidence is there in this painting that Bruegel was trying to make fun of barber-surgeons?

**b** From your knowledge of medicine in Early Modern Europe explain whether you think that Bruegel's criticisms are fair.

**c** Do you think that biased information like that in Source 1 can ever be of any value to a historian? Explain your answer.

**d** How important was Paré's work in the development of surgery?

You could include the following in your answer and other information of your own.

- The way that wounds were treated before Paré.
- Paré's treatment of wounds.
- Paré's writings.

**2** Between 400 BC and AD 1685 some things in medicine changed and some things stayed the same.

**a** Give examples of a number things which:

  i changed
  ii stayed the same.

**b** Were all the changes that took place examples of progress in medicine? Explain your answer.

**c** What part did the following play in bringing about change in medicine during this time:

  i brilliant individuals
  ii chance
  iii war?

**d** What factors hindered progress in medicine during this time? Give examples to support your answer.

**3** What do you think was the most important development in medicine during this time? Explain your answer.

# CHAPTER 10

# MEDICINE ON THE BRINK

## 10.1 The old order begins to change

The interest in science and experimentation continued into the 18th century. Physics became more established. The microscope had been invented as early as 1683 by the Dutchman, Anthony van Leeuwenhoek. This was now followed by the thermometer, invented by Fahrenheit in 1709 and Celsius in 1742. In chemistry a number of new substances were discovered such as hydrogen, oxygen, and nitrous oxide. These inventions and discoveries, however, did not make an impact on medicine until the 19th century.

Nevertheless, it was a time when old ideas about medicine were questioned. Physicians, such as Hermann Boerhaave, were stimulated into observing patients more closely and keeping accurate records (see box). Boerhaave also caused a new edition of Vesalius' work to be published, as many doctors were keen to increase their knowledge of anatomy. In physiology Albrecht van Haller, a student of Boerhaave's, investigated breathing and digestion. In the USA, in 1822, William Beaumont had a patient whose stomach was opened by gunshot. He was able to observe the digestive system at work. None of this, however, resulted in doctors discovering the real cause of disease.

There was also some important work in surgery, as well as the contribution of John Hunter (see box). William Cheselden (1688–1752) found a way of removing a stone from a bladder in just over a minute! Such speed was welcomed, given the lack of effective anaesthetics at this time.

### HERMANN BOERHAAVE

Hermann Boerhaave was the Professor of Medicine at Leyden, in Holland, between 1718 and 1729. He taught his students to keep case histories and carry out post-mortems to try to establish causes of death. He taught the need to make use of science and the experience of the patient rather than just rely on abstract theory. His students moved on to other parts of Europe and to America, spreading his ideas. One of these, Alexander Monro, turned Edinburgh University into a leading medical centre.

### JOHN HUNTER

John Hunter (1728–93) has been called the 'Father of Modern Surgery'. His brother, William, was a famous surgeon. John went to London to work for him in his dissecting rooms. He trained as a doctor. He worked as a surgeon in St George's Hospital and, for a time, became an army surgeon. He built up a collection of anatomical specimens from people and animals which formed the basis of the Royal College of Surgeons' collection. John invented new procedures, like **tracheotomy** to clear air passages. He also investigated transplanting teeth.

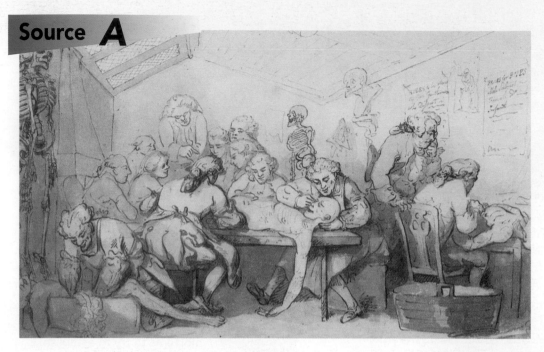

◀ In the 18th century, surgeons based their work on an increasing knowledge of anatomy and pathology. This drawing, by Thomas Rowlandson, shows William Hunter's dissecting room in the latter half of the 18th century.

The medical profession became more respected during the 18th century. Surgeons at last gained equal status with physicians. Organizations were set up in Britain and Europe to represent surgeons. The Company of Surgeons was established in 1745 and, in 1800, it became the Royal College of Surgeons of London. This set the standards for surgical training. People were beginning to feel that society should care for its members. Several new hospitals were founded at this time by rich people, including Guy's in 1721 and the Middlesex Hospital in 1745.

## 'Quackery'

Despite the search for new knowledge, many old ideas continued in use during the 18th century. Many doctors still clung to the four humours and their associated treatments. To explain the mystery of how disease spread, many adopted the idea of 'miasmas' (colourless, odourless gases in the air which spread infection). 'Quack' doctors, in search of profit, peddled all sorts of nonsense. For example, 'piss-prophets' emphasised diagnosis by examining urine. Other 'quacks' recommended useless pills or claimed that evil worms caused illness. A German doctor, Franz Mesmer (1734–1815), claimed that he could cure patients by hypnotism.

**Source B**

▶ This picture of doctors was drawn by William Hogarth, an 18th century artist. They are sniffing the gold tops of their walking sticks which contain a liquid they thought would prevent infection. One doctor is tasting some patient's urine.

## QUESTIONS

1  During the 18th century it was fashionable to question and inquire. What effect did this attitude have on medicine?

2  Despite this attitude why did many old ideas continue in use?

## 10.2 The situation in 1820

Despite the advances of the 17th and 18th centuries medical practice and knowledge was still limited.

- People still did not know what really caused disease. Doctors had an insufficient knowledge of chemistry and biochemistry. There was also a lack of technical aids for doctors. Although microscopes were in existence, they were not very powerful. Further developments in physics were needed if they were to be improved.

- Surgical operations were still carried out in filthy conditions as surgeons did not realize the need for cleanliness. Infection, therefore, was rife. Operations had to be carried out in haste because there were no effective anaesthetics. Patients often died from the trauma of the pain. Blood loss during an operation was another problem. Although surgeons knew there was a problem with losing too much blood, they were unable to carry out successful transfusions. They were not aware at this time that there were blood groups which had to be matched.

By the early 20th century, however, most of these problems had been overcome. How and why was this able to happen?

### THE GROWTH OF INDUSTRY

**First Phase: late-18th – 19th century**
- **1781** James Watt perfected the steam engine. This enabled machinery to be powered effectively. The need for new machinery meant the growth of an engineering industry.
- **1840s** Rapid extension of the railway network. Travel and communications quicker.
- **1850–75** Britain was the 'workshop of the world'. It was later challenged by the USA, Germany and France.

**Second Phase: late-19th century**
New light industries were developed:

- the motor car
- giant chemical firms
- electrical engineering
- new materials came into use such as steel, rubber and aluminium.

**Third Phase: 20th century**
Society moved into the age of high-technology. New machines invented to aid medicine. For example:

- **1896** X-ray machines
- **1945** kidney dialysis machine
- **1970** body scanners.

## 10.3 The impact of the Industrial Revolution

In the late-18th century a number of changes took place which turned Britain into an industrialized society. The population began to increase rapidly and there was an increase in demand for all types of goods. Factories that were full of machines sprang up. These machines were powered at first by water, then by steam and latterly by electricity.

Around the factories large towns grew up very rapidly. Initially this brought slum housing, poor public health and epidemics of infectious diseases.

On the other hand, industrialization stimulated the rapid development of the sciences and technology. New machines and new materials were brought into use. For example, a deeper knowledge of physics and improvements in glass-making led to the manufacture of more powerful microscopes. This, in turn, was a vital factor in scientists discovering that germs caused disease. Once this breakthrough was made new cures and vaccines followed.

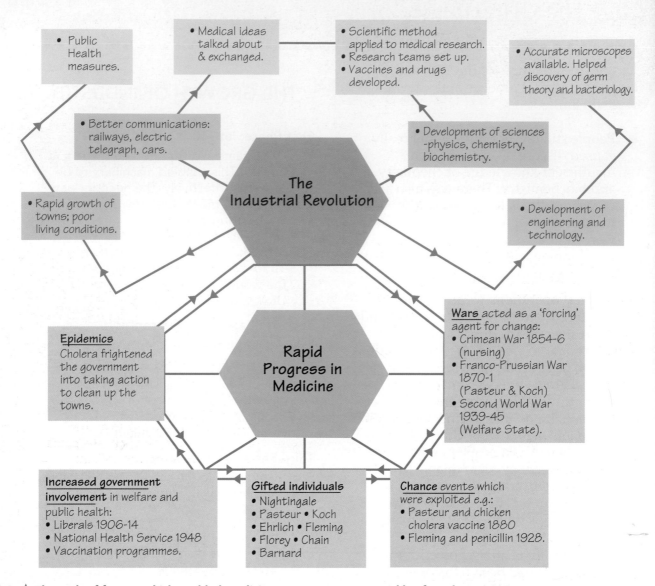

**▲ The web of factors which enabled medicine to progress very quickly after about 1850.**

Chemistry also made advances during this period. Chemists, working in teams, began research into drugs.

When electricity came into use in the late-19th century it opened the way for new machines and technical aids to help medicine.

As well as industrialization other factors were also at work (see diagram). Combinations of these factors enabled medicine to progress very quickly from the mid-19th century, compared with the slow pace of change over the previous 3000 years. This rapid progress – sometimes called the medical revolution – is dealt with in the next three chapters.

## QUESTIONS

1 What problems faced medicine in 1820?

2 Why has there been such rapid progress in medicine since about 1850?

3 Which of the factors in the diagram had influenced medicine before 1820? Give examples and details.

# CHAPTER 11

# THE FIGHT AGAINST INFECTIOUS DISEASE

## 11.1 Edward Jenner and smallpox

The first significant step in the fight against infectious disease was made in 1796, with the discovery of a vaccine to protect people from smallpox.

During the 18th century smallpox had taken over from the plague as the major killer disease. Victims suffered from a high fever and sores full of pus appeared all over the body. If the heart, brain and lungs became infected, death was certain. Some people who survived were left disfigured and, often, blinded. Many had tried to make themselves **immune** from smallpox by the risky practice of inoculation. This involved deliberately infecting themselves with the disease, taken from someone who was suffering from a mild form of it. By doing this they hoped that they would catch a mild form of smallpox too.

Edward Jenner (1749–1823) was a doctor from Berkeley in Gloucestershire. He studied under John Hunter, the famous surgeon, and from him learned the importance of scientific observation and experiment. Hunter once advised Jenner, 'don't think, try the experiment'. Jenner was aware of the local belief that milkmaids who suffered from the mild disease of cowpox, never caught the dreaded smallpox. Years of observation confirmed this belief. So, in 1796, he decided to move on from observation to experiment. For the experiment to work he had to use a person who had never had cowpox or smallpox. He chose a young boy, James Phipps, and injected him with pus from the sores of Sarah Nelmes, a milkmaid with cowpox. Phipps developed cowpox. When he was fully recovered, Jenner gave him a dose of smallpox. If the experiment worked all would be well. If not, Phipps would develop smallpox and probably die.

The experiment worked (see Source A). Jenner had found a way to make people immune from a deadly, infectious disease without the risks of inoculation. He called his method vaccination, after the Latin word *vacca* which means 'cow'.

### INOCULATION

Lady Mary Wortley Montagu learned of inoculation against smallpox when she was in Turkey with her husband, the British ambassador. In 1718 she introduced the idea into England. A cut

was made in the patient's arm and a thread soaked in pus from the sores of a victim who had a mild form of the disease was drawn through. The patient was kept in a warm room until the symptoms had disappeared. Inoculation became popular but some patients died as they contracted a fatal form of the disease. Inoculation houses were set up and some doctors, like William Woodville, became famous and wealthy from the technique.

## Source A

I selected a healthy boy, [James Phipps] about eight-years old. The cowpox matter was inserted into the arm of the boy on 14 May 1796. On the seventh day he complained of uneasiness, on the ninth day he became a little chilly, lost his appetite and had a slight headache but next day he was perfectly well. Then he was inoculated with smallpox, but no disease followed.

▲ **Edward Jenner, writing about his vaccination experiment in 1798.**

## The reaction to Jenner's discovery

Despite the success of Jenner's experiments, some doctors were against vaccination. This was because they either did not want to accept new ideas or they had a vested interest in supporting inoculation. They had become rich and famous from this technique and feared that they would lose everything to the new methods of an unknown country doctor. Jenner, however, had powerful supporters. Some members of the royal family were vaccinated. Vaccination was widely accepted abroad. A group of Native Americans travelled to Britain to thank Jenner. In 1813 the Emperor Napoleon released a prisoner of war at Jenner's request. 'Ah, it's Jenner, I can refuse Jenner nothing!' the Emperor said. In 1802 Parliament gave Jenner £10,000 and in 1806 a further £20,000. In 1840 vaccination was made free for all infants and, in 1853, it was made compulsory. This was especially surprising at a time when the government usually refused to interfere in people's lives, even for the good of their health. Smallpox was on the way to being defeated, even though nobody had the faintest idea how vaccination worked. It was to be 80 years before another vaccine was discovered.

## Source B

27 October 1793 – John Moore Paget was inoculated with smallpox.

26 January 1834 – Baby Margaret was vaccinated by Mr Drake, the smallpox being at Mells and Downhead.

25 June 1844 – Jane did not go out on account of Richard who was not so well, but leeches and warm baths relieved him.

▲ Extracts from the unpublished diaries of the Paget family of Cranmore, Somerset.

▼ This cartoon, drawn by James Gillray in 1802, shows the supposed fears of some people at the time about Jenner's use of cowpox matter as a vaccine against smallpox.

## Source C

## Source D

In August 1799 John Ring from Wincanton in Somerset met Dr Jenner. In 1808 he went to Ringwood, Hampshire, to investigate supposed failures of vaccination. Feelings ran so high that his group had to carry pistols for defence. When the British Vaccine Establishment was opened in 1809, Ring was the principal vaccinator. He vaccinated so many that Jenner, speaking of a lady who had vaccinated ten thousand people, said that it was nothing compared to honest John Ring.

▲ From *The History of Wincanton* by George Sweetman, 1903.

## Source E

After being vaccinated with cowpox she was so ill with fever, and with these boils, that she could not work for a week. Many years later she caught smallpox.

▲ An account by C. Cooke, an apothecary from Gloucester, of a patient whose vaccination failed to give protection from smallpox, 1799.

## Source F

This day is published, price one shilling [5p], a letter from John Birch, Esquire. In this publication it is noticed that there was a Parliamentary grant of £30,000 to Dr Jenner for an unsuccessful experiment. There is also a letter proving the production of a new and fatal disease called the 'vaccine ulcer' described by Astley Cooper, Esquire, surgeon of Guy's Hospital. There is a letter from Mr Westcott of Ringwood proving the failures of the experiment there. A list of those who died of cow pox there. A list of those who were defectively [ineffectively] vaccinated and caught smallpox; and those who died of smallpox after having been vaccinated and told that they would be protected. There is also a list of other failures under the Treatment of the Jennerian Institution.

▲ Opposition to Jenner and the smallpox vaccination shown in a contemporary letter.

## Source G

Medicine has never before produced any single improvement of such usefulness. You have erased from the list of human afflictions one of the greatest. Future generations will only know through history that the loathsome smallpox has existed and has been wiped out by you.

▲ A letter to Edward Jenner from Thomas Jefferson, President of the USA, 1802.

## SUMMARY

▶ Smallpox was a feared epidemic disease in the 18th century.

▶ Inoculation was introduced into Britain by Lady Mary Wortley Montagu. Though popular, it was risky and did not reduce the toll from smallpox.

▶ Jenner saw that cowpox victims became immune from smallpox.

▶ He vaccinated people with cowpox which made them immune to the disease.

▶ Opposition was overcome because vaccination worked, was widely publicized and had many supporters.

▶ Jenner had no idea how or why vaccination worked, so his work did not lead directly to other developments.

## QUESTIONS

1 Study Source B. How does it show
  a change and
  b continuity in medical practice?

2 What factors led to Jenner's success with the smallpox vaccine?

3 a Describe what is shown in Source C.
  b Would a historian find this source useful?

4 a Why was there opposition to vaccination?
  b How was this opposition overcome?

5 Was Jenner's discovery a change or a development in the history of medicine? Explain your answer.

### Spontaneous generation

By 1800 most scientists and doctors knew that micro-organisms called germs or microbes existed, but many of them thought germs were the *result* of disease, not the *cause* of it. This idea was called spontaneous generation. Some believed that disease was caused by gases, called miasmas, others believed different theories, but none of them thought germs were the cause.

### Pasteur and the germ theory

Louis Pasteur was the scientist who made the first links between germs and disease. He did not set out to do this. His research was driven by the needs of businesses that asked him to solve a particular problem. In 1857 he began to investigate a problem in the brewing industry. Sugar beet, used to make alcohol, often went sour during fermentation and could not be used. Pasteur examined samples of the sour liquid under a microscope. He thought the souring was caused by germs in the air. He proved this by experimenting with water in a swan-neck flask. When the water was heated the warm air was pushed out of the flask around the bend in the neck. The curved neck then trapped the air and the germs it carried. When the neck was broken the air (and germs) rushed in and decay set in. When this discovery was announced many scientists and doctors refused to believe it. Even when Pasteur successfully carried out the experiment in public, some of them still clung to the spontaneous generation theory. Other doctors and scientists saw he had made a definite link between germs and decay.

In 1865 Pasteur began to study *pébrine,* a silkworm disease. His studies were disrupted by the deaths of his father and two of his daughters but, by 1867, he was able to demonstrate that germs were the cause of *pébrine.* The link between germs and disease had been made.

## Source H

I place some liquid in a flask with a long neck. I boil it and let it cool. In a few days little animals will grow in it. But by boiling it I had killed the germs. If I repeat the experiment but draw the neck into a curve, but still open, the liquid will remain pure for three or four years. What difference is there between them? They both contain the same liquid and they both contain air. It is that in one the dust in the air and its germs can fall in, in the other they cannot. I have kept germs out of it and, therefore, have kept Life from it – for Life is a germ and a germ is Life.

▲ **Pasteur's description of the experiment he carried out in public at the University of Paris on 7 April 1864.**

Louis Pasteur was a French chemist. In 1849 he was made Professor of Chemistry at Strasbourg, and in 1854 he moved to Lille. He was the first person to prove the connection between germs and decay and then the connection between germs and disease.

Pasteur made many of his investigations for businesses who had problems that were losing them money. His researches were not always continuous. His work on silkworm disease, begun in 1865, was interrupted by deaths in his family. In 1868 a brain haemorrhage left him paralysed on one side. He stopped working, but by 1877 he was back, investigating anthrax.

His investigations of animal diseases had good results. He discovered vaccines for chicken cholera (1880), anthrax (1881) and rabies (1885). The deaths of two of his daughters from typhoid fever may have started his investigations into human disease. He tried to produce a cholera vaccine as early as 1865, but failed. In 1888 the French government set up the *Institut Pasteur,* for Pasteur and others to further medical research.

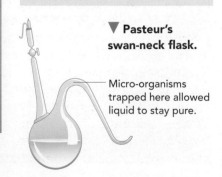

▼ **Pasteur's swan-neck flask.**

Micro-organisms trapped here allowed liquid to stay pure.

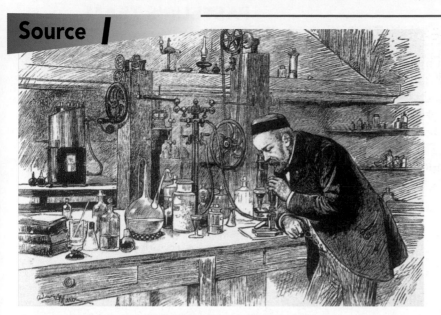

▲ This contemporary engraving shows Pasteur working in his laboratory. This was produced when Pasteur had become famous as a chemist.

# 11.3 Robert Koch

• • • • • • • • • • • • • • • • • • • • • • • • • • • • •

By 1870, Pasteur had shown the connection between germs and decay and disease. The next step, linking a particular germ or microbe to a particular disease, was made by a German doctor, Robert Koch, who had the detailed medical knowledge that Pasteur, a chemist, lacked. In 1872 Koch began to study anthrax, a fatal disease which affected cattle and sheep. It could spread to humans. By 1875 he had identified the microbe by studying the blood of affected and unaffected animals.

Koch moved on to study the germ that caused blood poisoning and septicemia in wounds. This microbe was impossible to see at first, even with a microscope. New technology came to his aid. He used new industrial dyes to stain the microbe. Now it could be seen. He devised a way to grow the germs and then used his daughter's pet mice to experiment with the germ. Soon Koch had a fluid that contained only one kind of germ. Mice injected with the fluid developed septicemia. Koch knew he had to *prove* he had the right germ. Again, new technology helped. He connected a new kind of lens to his microscope and photographed the whole process.

Koch developed superb experimental methods. As well as the use of dyes and photography, he developed a **solid culture** to breed colonies of germs on. This was more reliable than Pasteur's liquid culture. Koch went on to isolate other germs. In 1882 he discovered the germ that caused tuberculosis (TB) and in 1883 he identified the germ that caused cholera.

## ROBERT KOCH
### (1843–1910)

Robert Koch was born near Hanover. He graduated in medicine from Gottingen University and went to work in Hamburg in 1866. He joined the Prussian army in the war against France in 1870. The French were beaten within six months. After that he became the medical officer in Wollstein, a town near the border with Poland. His wife bought him a microscope for his 29th birthday. It was to affect his life greatly. He went on to be a pioneer of the new science of bacteriology, proving that one specific germ could cause a particular disease in animals and humans. He identified the microbes which caused TB (1882) and cholera (1883). His work caused the German government to set up the Institute for Infectious Diseases in Berlin in 1891. Koch won the Nobel prize in 1905 for his work.

▼ Robert Koch is shown as St George defeating tuberculosis.

## Microbe hunters

The work of Pasteur and Koch meant that the real cause of disease was known at last. Pasteur's advice to 'seek the microbe' was followed and the new science of bacteriology was established. 'Microbe hunters' became the stars of scientific research. The chart below lists some of the other microbes (or germs) which were found.

| Year | Microbe discovered | Name of scientist |
|------|--------------------|-------------------|
| 1879 | Leprosy | Hansen |
| 1880 | Typhoid | Eberth |
| 1882 | Diphtheria | Klebs |
| 1884 | Tetanus | Nicholaier |
| 1884 | Pneumonia | Frankael |
| 1894 | Plague | Kitasato and Yersin |

The discovery of specific microbes led on to the production of vaccines and, later, the pioneering of chemotherapy. The mass murderers of earlier times were being controlled.

# 11.4 Vaccines

## Chicken cholera

Pasteur read of Koch's achievements. He was determined to make more discoveries, to win prestige for France which had lost land to Germany at the end of the Franco-Prussian war of 1870–1. Pasteur built up a research team and, in 1877, began work on the anthrax germ. In 1880 he was asked to stop work on anthrax and investigate chicken cholera, a disease that was sweeping through the chicken population and losing French poultry farmers a lot of money. Pasteur and his team needed a liquid culture that the germ (already isolated by the professor of a veterinary school in Toulouse) would grow in. The usual liquids, water, urine, yeast, did not work. A sterile broth of chicken gristle and potash did. Now the disease had to be passed on to other chickens. One of Pasteur's team, Charles Chamberland, was responsible for injecting the chickens.

## PASTEUR'S TEAM

Charles Chamberland (left) was one of the scientists who were attracted to work in Pasteur's team. Often they gave up more comfortable careers elsewhere to take part. Others included Emile Roux, who discovered the diphtheria toxin, Alexander Yersin, the Swiss scientist, who discovered the bubonic plague **bacillus**, and Albert Calmette, who became director of the Pasteur Institute, and, together with Camille Gurin, found the vaccine for tuberculosis.

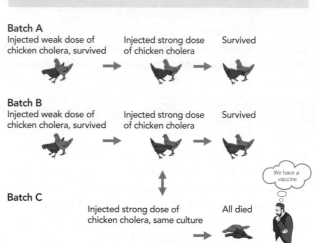

▲ How Pasteur discovered the principle of making vaccines from the germs of the disease chicken cholera.

Pasteur gave Chamberland the liquid culture, but Chamberland, who was going on holiday, forgot to inject the chickens. The liquid stood uncovered on the bench for many days. Chamberland injected the chickens when he returned, but they did not die. He told Pasteur what had happened. Pasteur told him to inject the chickens with a fresh, strong culture. The chickens still did not die. Pasteur left a culture exposed to air for several days. New chickens were injected with this culture and did not die. Pasteur then injected these chickens and a new batch with a fresh culture. The new chickens died. Those who had been injected with the exposed culture did not. The germs had been weakened by exposure to air. They were not strong enough to kill, but they were strong enough to give immunity to a strong dose. This is the principle of **attenuation**. Pasteur called this culture 'vaccine' as a tribute to Jenner.

## Anthrax – the experiment at Pouilly-le-Fort

After the discovery of the chicken cholera vaccine Pasteur was determined to try and find a vaccine for anthrax. His team, led by Dr Emile Roux, managed to produce a weakened strain of anthrax by keeping the germs at a temperature of 42–3°C over a period of eight days.

In 1881 Monsieur Rossignol, a French journalist, challenged Pasteur to test out the vaccine in public. Pasteur accepted and the tests were set for 5 May on Rossignol's farm at Pouilly-le-Fort, near Paris. The event attracted huge interest throughout Europe and was attended by politicians, farmers and journalists. Pasteur was provided with sixty sheep, twenty-five of which would be vaccinated and then given deadly anthrax germs. Another twenty-five would just be given a fatal dose of anthrax. The remaining ten sheep were left alone so that they could be compared with any survivors. The experiment was carried out. By 2 June the unvaccinated sheep were dead and those that had been vaccinated were fit and well. It was a complete triumph. Reports of the event were sent by electric telegraph on the very same day. The world soon knew of Pasteur's success (see Source L). Robert Koch also tried to find a vaccine for anthrax, but failed. He resorted to attacking Pasteur in the medical press.

Pasteur's vaccine greatly reduced the death rate from anthrax in animals and saved the French farming industry large amounts of money.

These experiments on animals were important in human medicine too. Once people were confident that vaccination worked on animals they were more likely to accept human vaccination. Also, the techniques and equipment developed would be the same whether the patient was a chicken, a sheep or a person.

## Source K

Will you have some microbe? There is some everywhere. Microbiolatry [the worship of microbes] is the fashion, it reigns undisputed; it is a doctrine which must not even be discussed, especially when its Pontiff [Pope], the learned Monsieur Pasteur, has pronounced the holy words, 'I have spoken.' The microbe alone is and shall be the characteristic of a disease; that is understood and settled; the microbe alone is true, and Pasteur is its prophet.

▲ The article in the *Veterinary Press*, 31 January, 1881, in which Monsieur Rossignol ridiculed the germ theory and which led to the challenge at Pouilly-le-Fort.

## Source L

Paris 2 June. 9.30pm [by telegraph from our correspondents]

Today I went to Pouilly-le-Fort to see the result of an experiment by M. Pasteur . . . On 5 May, 25 sheep were marked with a hole in their ear and inoculated with [anthrax vaccine]. On 31 May all 50 sheep were inoculated with the strongest [anthrax] virus. M. Pasteur predicted that today [2 June] the sheep not inoculated with the vaccine would be dead and the others would show no symptoms of sickness. As M. Pasteur foretold at two o'clock 23 sheep were dead. Two more died an hour later. The sheep which had been vaccinated frolicked and gave signs of perfect health. Farmers now know that a perfect prevention exists against anthrax.

▲ A report from *The Times*, Friday 3 June 1881, describing Pasteur's anthrax experiment at Pouilly-le-Fort.

## QUESTIONS

1 Did the hostility between Pasteur and Koch help or hinder progress? Explain your answer.

2 How did communications such as railways, the press and electric telegraph, help medical progress?

## Rabies

In 1882 Pasteur's team got set to produce a vaccine for rabies, a terrible disease that is always fatal once symptoms develop. Emile Roux made most progress in early studies, devising a way of drying rabbits' spines in a glass flask to see how long the rabies virus remained dangerous. Pasteur saw this and copied Roux's idea. It caused a furious row, but Pasteur began to test the vaccine on animals. He administered a series of injections starting with spines that had been drying for fourteen days which would not pass the disease on. The next injection was made using a thirteen day old spine and so on until the last injection used a fresh spine which would definitely cause the disease. This gradual increase of virulent germs resulted in immunity. The team, and Pasteur himself, had doubts about this method but, in 1885, their hand was forced by a chance happening. A mother turned up at Pasteur's laboratory on 6 July. She had come from Alsace with her son who was covered in bites from a rabid dog. Joseph Meister was doomed unless Pasteur tried the untested vaccine. Dr Vulpian and Dr Grancher advised Pasteur to try. The boy was given a series of injections, which proved to be successful (Source N).

## Diphtheria

The diphtheria bacillus was discovered by a German doctor, Edwin Klebs. Freidrich Loeffler bred them but could not work out how they killed. He guessed that they produced some kind of toxin or poison. The search was taken up by Roux who was able to prove that it was the toxin, not the germs, that was fatal. Emil von Behring, a former member of Koch's team, developed a serum from the blood of animals that survived the disease, which he called 'anti-toxin'. Once injected, this prevented the bacillus from producing toxin within the body. The disease was conquered not by one person but by several, all building upon the discoveries of the others.

## Tuberculosis

Koch tested a vaccine for tuberculosis (TB), called 'tuberculin', which seemed to work on animals. The German government pushed him to announce the success at the 10th International Medical Congress in 1890. It caused great excitement and thousands of sufferers flocked to Berlin for treatment. Tuberculin, however, did not work and Koch was blamed. His career waned but his team continued to succeed.

## Government help

The governments of France and Germany realized how the work of Pasteur and Koch brought national prestige. Both men were given research institutes to carry out their work.

## Source M

▲ Removing saliva from a rabid dog. This engraving shows the risks taken by Pasteur's team.

## Source N

Joseph Meister, aged nine years, was bitten on 4 July, at eight o'clock in the morning. This child had been knocked over by the dog and showed numerous bites, on the hands, legs and thighs, some so deep as to make walking difficult. The dog was certainly rabid. Joseph Meister had been pulled out from him covered in foam and blood. The death of this child being certain, I decided to try the method which had been successful with dogs. Young Meister was inoculated under a fold of skin with half a syringeful of the spinal cord of a rabbit which had died of rabies and had been preserved for fifteen days in a flask of dry air. Joseph Meister has survived not only the rabies from the bites but also the rabies with which I inoculated him.

▲ Pasteur's description of the rabies injection, from *A Lecture on the Prevention of Rabies*, 1885.

## Industry, science & technology

- The much improved microscope allowed bacteria to be studied.
- Koch used industrial chemical dyes to stain bacteria.

## Communications

- The results of experiments and research were spread quickly via telegraph, newspapers and journals. Railways enabled scientists to meet regularly.

## Research techniques

- Both Pasteur and Koch devised experiments to prove theories.
- Both had research teams.

Factors which enabled Pasteur and Koch to succeed

## Personal qualities

- Both men were intelligent, persistent and determined.
- Both spoke in public at the risk of abuse from doubters.

## Chance events

- Chamberland's 'mistake' when Pasteur was researching a vaccine for chicken cholera.
- The surprise arrival of Joseph Meister allowed Pasteur to test his rabies vaccine on humans.

## War

- The Franco-Prussian War (1870–1) ended in a disastrous defeat for the French. Tension between the two countries followed.
- Pasteur and Koch were spurred on by this tension. They became rivals; a new discovery brought prestige for their country.

# QUESTIONS

1 Look back through this chapter and list the achievements of Pasteur and Koch with their dates.

2 a What was the germ theory of disease?

  b Explain how the germ theory opened the way for further progress in medicine.

  c Why did some people oppose the germ theory?

3 What personal qualities did Pasteur and Koch have which enabled them to succeed in their research?

4 Did chance play a part in the production of vaccines? Explain your answer.

5 Out of all the factors which enabled Pasteur and Koch to succeed, which do you think was the most important?

6 Study Source J on page 85 and Source M on page 88. Why do you think such pictures were made?

# SUMMARY

▶ In 1850 there were still several different ideas about what caused disease.

▶ Pasteur was asked by Monsieur Bigo to explain why his alcohol fermentation had gone bad. His experiments showed that germs caused decay.

▶ Pasteur demonstrated that germs caused disease in animals.

▶ Robert Koch was able to prove that each type of germ caused a specific disease by his work on anthrax.

▶ A variety of factors enabled these pioneers to make their discoveries.

● Both Pasteur and Koch built teams of scientists and doctors to help their developments.

● Individual genius enabled them to recognize opportunities for progress.

● Development did not happen in isolation. Communications enabled pioneers to improve upon each other's discoveries.

## 11.5  Drugs and infectious disease

### Progress in the fight against infectious diseases by 1900

By 1900 the germs which caused the most common diseases had been discovered. Koch, Pasteur and others had developed a number of vaccines that could prevent people from catching these diseases. Governments were also introducing preventative measures against disease by enforcing councils to provide clean water and efficient sewage disposal. Doctors and scientists now needed to find effective cures for people with infectious disease.

There was some knowledge to build on. Drugs made from natural substances had been used for centuries in the treatment of illness. For example, opium was used as a pain-killer and colocynth as a purgative. These drugs, however, were unable to combat the bacteria which caused the disease. By about 1890, the work of Joseph Lister was accepted by most doctors. Lister showed that a chemical, carbolic acid, would kill germs outside the body – but it was too toxic to use internally. A chemical that could be used safely to kill bacteria inside a person was needed. In 1900 the conditions were ripe for a breakthrough in curative medicine to be made – but who was going to make it?

### Paul Ehrlich

By the late-19th century, the German chemical industry was progressing rapidly, particularly in the manufacture of synthetic dyes. Koch was experienced in using synthetic textile dyes to stain microbes for examination under the microscope. This made the microbes stand out and easier to study.

Paul Ehrlich was a German doctor who joined Koch's research team in 1889. He began by working with Emil Behring on diptheria and became fascinated by the fact that the body produced **antibodies** to ward off specific germs inside a person without damaging the rest of the body. He referred to such antibodies as magic bullets because, like a bullet from a gun, they sought out their specific target. Antibodies, however, did not always kill off invasive bacteria. Ehrlich began to think that there must be a chemical dye that could be used internally to kill specific bacteria without harming the rest of the body – a synthetic magic bullet.

### The search for a magic bullet

Ehrlich became director of his own research institute. His team concentrated on looking for chemical cures for disease. In 1899 Ehrlich, and his team of researchers, started to test different dyes to see if they would kill microbes. This involved a great deal of patience and perseverance. Numerous dyes were tried but they met with only limited success. Dyes were found that attacked malaria and sleeping sickness germs.

## PAUL EHRLICH

Ehrlich was born in the town of Strehlen in Silesia, Germany, in 1854. He studied at the University of Leipzig, researching in chemistry and bacteriology. He worked first as a doctor but, in 1886, caught tuberculosis (TB). It took him three years to recover completely. In 1889, he joined Robert Koch's research team at the Institute for Infectious Diseases in Berlin. He helped Emil Behring to find an anti-toxin that cured diphtheria. From 1899, until his death in 1915, he was the Director of the Royal Institute of Experimental Therapy in Frankfurt. It was here that he carried out his research into chemotherapy (the treatment of disease by chemical drugs). In 1908 he shared the Nobel Prize for medicine with the Russian bacteriologist Elie Metchnikov.

**Industry**
Progress in the chemical industry provided Ehrlich with the idea that chemicals (e.g. synthetic dyes) might be able to kill germs inside the body.

**Personal Qualities**
Ehrlich was determined and skilful. He was inspired by Koch and Behring.

**Science and Technology**
Improved knowledge of physics and skilled engineering provided Ehrlich with technical aids (e.g. the microscope).

**Research Techniques**
Teamwork and careful observation were crucial. Hata had the patience to re-check previous work.

◀ **Factors involved in the discovery of Salvarsan 606.**

## The syphilis microbe

In 1906 the microbe that caused syphilis was identified by Fritz Schaudinn and Paul Erich Hoffman. Syphilis was a sexually transmitted disease which killed thousands of people each year. In 1907 Ehrlich decided to test chemical compounds of various poisons, hoping that one might kill the syphilis germ. His team made up and tested over 600 **arsenic** compounds. All of them were said to be useless. The research seemed to be going down a blind alley.

In 1909 Sahachiro Hata, a Japanese bacteriologist, joined Ehrlich's team. Hata was asked to retest the compounds already discarded. He found that compound 606 did in fact kill the syphilis germ. Why had it previously been ruled out? Perhaps the assistant who had previously tested the compound lacked concentration or was not such a skilled researcher. Ehrlich called the new drug Salvarsan 606. He was concerned that doctors might give the wrong dose, or that the drug might be harmful in other ways. He insisted on repeated testing on many hundreds of animals that were deliberately infected with syphilis. He found that it always targeted the syphilis germ without harming the rest of the body. Salvarsan 606 was used for the first time on a human patient in 1911.

## Opposition

The discovery of Salvarsan 606 was not welcomed by everyone. Some doctors were not keen to use the new drug; it was not very soluble and was difficult and painful to inject into veins. Some doctors believed that people would become promiscuous now that they knew that syphilis could be cured. Despite Ehrlich's rigorous testing there were many doctors who did not like the idea of giving their patients arsenic, in any form.

# QUESTIONS

1 a What progress had been made in the fight against infectious diseases by 1900?

   b What new breakthrough was needed?

2 a What factors enabled the discovery of Salvarsan 606 to be made?

   b Was any one of these factors more important than the others? Explain your answer.

3 a What opposition was there to Salvarsan 606?

   b Does your study of the history of medicine make you surprised that there was opposition to such an important breakthrough in the treatment of disease? Give reasons and examples in your answer.

### Gerhard Domagk and sulphonamide drugs

Domagk worked for a large chemical firm in Elberfeld, Germany. Inspired by Ehrlich's work, he carried out a programme of systematic research looking for dyes that might destroy infecting microbes within the body. Domagk, like Ehrlich, was conscientious and determined.

His first success was the discovery of germanin, a drug which was effective against sleeping sickness. Then, in 1932, he discovered that a red dye, called prontosil, stopped the streptococcus microbe (which causes blood-poisoning) from multiplying in mice without harming the rest of the animal. He had no idea, however, whether this drug would work on humans. One day, in 1935, Domagk's daughter, Hildegarde, pricked herself with an infected needle and blood-poisoning set in. The girl was seriously ill and Domagk, with nothing to lose, gave her a huge dose of prontosil. Although her skin turned slightly red she made a rapid recovery.

Further research by a team of French scientists found that the compound in the dye which acted on the germs was sulphonamide, a chemical derived from coal tar. It was not long before other sulphonamide-derived drugs were developed that were capable of fighting diseases such as tonsillitis, puerperal fever and scarlet fever. In 1938, chemists working for the British firm, May and Baker, discovered a sulphonamide-derived drug that worked against the microbe causing pneumonia. They tried the drug on a Norfolk farm labourer, who had severe pneumonia, and it worked. They called the drug M&B 693, as it was the 693rd compound they tested before they met with success.

Sulphonamide drugs, however, had disadvantages. They sometimes caused damage to the kidneys and liver and were ineffective against the more virulent microbes. An even more powerful magic bullet was needed if infectious disease was to be conquered.

**Source O**

◄ A painting from the 1860s called *An Anxious Hour*. Before sulphonamide drugs, many children died of common illnesses such as 'flu.

## The story of penicillin

Penicillin was the world's first **antibiotic** – that is the first drug derived from living organisms, such as fungi, which would kill or prevent bacteria from growing. Penicillin was effective against a variety of germs. Its development involved three brilliant individuals: Alexander Fleming, Howard Florey and Ernst Chain.

### 'Alexander Fleming: The man who didn't invent penicillin'

The name Alexander Fleming is one of the most famous in the history of medicine. If you ask people what he did they will probably tell you that he 'invented penicillin' or perhaps they will say that he was 'the first person to discover penicillin'. Unfortunately, neither of these is true. Penicillin is not something you invent, it is a natural substance. For example, when cheese or fruit goes bad, mould grows on it. This mould has a Latin name 'penicillium' and has become more commonly known as penicillin. In 1871 Joseph Lister, who discovered antiseptic surgery, began experimenting with penicillium when he noticed that it appeared to weaken the microbes he was studying at the time.

## Source P

In 1881 a young nurse, working at King's College Hospital, was injured in a street accident. Her wound became infected. Several antiseptics were used, but unsuccessfully. Then a different treatment was used. It was so effective that she wrote down its name. It was 'penicillium'.

▲ Adapted from a book about Fleming published in 1985.

For reasons which we do not know, Lister did not continue his studies into penicillium and did not leave detailed notes on his work. Several other scientists also worked on using penicillium as a treatment, but were unable to find a way of making sufficient quantities to treat patients successfully. So there had been plenty of work done on penicillin before Fleming, but it was he who was to become famous. Why was this?

# ALEXANDER FLEMING
**Medical Researcher**

Born: Lochfield Ayrshire 1881.

Career: joined military services but resigned in 1901 when left money in a relative's will. Studied at St Mary's Hospital London and qualified as doctor in 1906.

Offered a job as a research assistant by Sir Almroth Wright, head of the Inoculation Department at St. Mary's Hospital.

Worked in a military hospital in Boulogne, France during the First World War.

Returned to St Mary's Hospital after the war and continued work as a medical researcher.

Honours won: knighted in 1944 (became Sir Alexander Fleming).

Won Nobel Prize for Medicine in 1945 (along with Florey and Chain).

Died: 1955.

## Fleming's discovery

During his time working in a military hospital in Boulogne, Fleming had been appalled to see that antiseptics such as carbolic acid did not prevent infection in deep wounds. Later in his memoirs he wrote 'Surrounded by all those men suffering and dying, I was consumed by a desire to discover something which would kill the microbes'. After the war, Fleming returned to St Mary's determined to find a substance that could kill germs more effectively. In 1922 he discovered that a natural substance in tears, lysozyme, would kill some germs, but not those that caused disease and infection.

## A chance discovery?

In 1928 Fleming was carrying out research into staphylococci (the germs which turn wounds septic). This involved growing the germs on **agar** in culture dishes. When Fleming came to clean a pile of discarded culture dishes, he noticed a mould spore had lodged itself on to one of them. It had grown to a size of about one centimetre across the dish. This was not an unusual thing to happen but Fleming was quick to notice that, around the mould, the germs had stopped growing. Another less astute person might have thrown away the dish and thought nothing more about it, but Fleming was curious. The mould was a member of the *penicilium notatum* family. It produced a bacteria killing juice which Fleming called penicillin.

He grew further quantities of the mould and found that it stopped other deadly germs growing, including anthrax and diphtheria bacilli. He injected it into animals without it harming them. However, if penicillin was to be of any practical use in treating humans, a way had to be found of turning the mould juice into a pure drug. Fleming and his colleagues were unable to do this. No one was prepared to give them the specialist help or money to carry out further experiments. Fleming wrote up his findings and published articles in the *British Journal of Experimental Pathology* in 1929 and 1931. He did nothing more about his discovery.

## Source Q

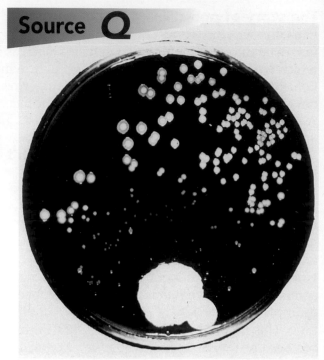

▲ The dish with the 'abnormal' culture that caught Fleming's attention. The mould can be seen at the bottom. At the top, germs can be seen growing in large numbers, but near the mould there is a clear area.

## Source R

Nothing is more certain than that when, in September 1928, I saw bacteria fading away from around the mould, I had no suspicion that I had got the clue to the most powerful substance yet used to defeat bacterial infection.

▲ Part of a speech made by Fleming in 1943.

## QUESTIONS

1 'The work of Fleming in penicillin came about more because of luck than individual brilliance.' Explain how far you agree with this statement.

2 If Fleming's discovery of the value of penicillin was so important, why didn't he develop the drug further?

## Howard Florey and Ernst Chain

In 1935 Howard Florey, an Australian doctor, became the head of the William Dunn School of Pathology at Oxford. He built up a team of brilliant biochemists to carry out medical research, including Ernst Chain, a scientist who was a refugee from Germany. Chain, who was Jewish, came to Britain to escape from Nazi persecution. In 1938 Florey's team decided to study germ-killing substances. Chain came across Fleming's articles on penicillin and they decided to see if they could produce pure penicillin from the mould juice. They succeeded in making small quantities of pure penicillin in powder form and decided to test it out on animals. On 25 May 1940 eight mice were injected with streptococci. Four were then given regular doses of penicillin and they survived. The other four mice all died within sixteen hours. Florey claimed that they had witnessed a miracle.

When you think that Florey was usually a very unexcitable man, you can understand how important he considered the experiment to be! You get a much better idea of how careful he was not to be carried away with optimism when you realise that a little later, when he had thought more about the experiment, he said 'But a man is three thousand times as big as a mouse'.

## Source S

People sometimes think that we worked on penicillin because we were interested in helping suffering humanity. I don't think that it ever entered our minds about suffering humanity. This was an interesting scientific exercise.

▲ **A comment made by Howard Florey in an interview in 1957.**

## QUESTIONS

1 Are you surprised by what Howard Florey says in Source S? Explain your answer.

2 Does what Florey said make you respect him less? Explain your answer.

## Problems in the production of pure penicillin

Florey's team did not have the resources to manufacture the pure penicillin in large amounts. They grew the mould in milk bottles, bed pans and milk churns and turned it into pure penicillin using a a process of freeze-drying devised by Chain. In October 1940 they tried it out for the first time on a human – a policeman, Albert Alexander, who was suffering from blood-poisoning and close to death. He began to recover after receiving penicillin, only to die when supplies ran out.

## War and the US chemical industry

The curative qualities of the drug were now beyond question. But mass producing the drug for commercial use still remained a problem. Only large chemical companies, with their resources could solve the problem, but it was unlikely they would be willing to get involved. By this time, Britain was deeply engaged in the Second World War against the might of Nazi Germany. The British chemical industry was too busy producing explosives to become involved in the manufacture of penicillin.

Florey realized that penicillin would be able to cure the deep infections caused by war wounds. He decided to visit the USA to try and persuade American chemical firms to invest in the mass production of penicillin. To begin with, he was unsuccessful. Then, in December 1941, the USA entered the war after the Japanese attacked Pearl Harbour. Soon, the US government had made grants available to firms wishing to buy expensive equipment to make penicillin. Mass production by British firms began in 1943. When the Allies launched the D-day invasion of Europe there was sufficient penicillin to treat all the wounded and thousands of lives were saved. In 1945 the Americans estimated that almost a sixth of all wounded men were saved. They were given penicillin to avoid death from infected wounds. After the war more efficient processes for the mass production of penicillin were invented. The cost of the drug was reduced and it became used across the world to treat a whole range of diseases.

## Factors in the development of penicillin

When you answer questions in the exam on the development of penicillin, you may well be asked to consider how important certain *factors* were in helping make it successful.

Let us look at some of those factors and consider what you might say in the exam if you were asked 'how far' each of them played a part. (Don't forget that if you are asked how far one of the factors was important, you not only have to explain the importance of that factor, but how important the others were too.)

### Chance (or luck)

This is the factor that is usually associated with Fleming's discovery. Certainly you can say that chance played a part because Fleming had not been looking for penicillin and had only found the mould by chance. But was it really chance? If Fleming had not been carrying out medical research, or if he had been a less observant person then he might not have noticed the mould. So you could say it was the result of individual ability, not chance.

### War and governments

War had a big part to play in the development of penicillin because the British and US governments put large sums of money into mass producing penicillin. Without this the drug would not have reached most of the people it saved. But Fleming didn't do his research because of war (although he was motivated by what he saw in the First World War) and Florey and Chain said they did their work because they enjoyed the science. So once again it's not so straightforward.

### Individuals and teams

Obviously Fleming, Florey and Chain were very important in developing medicine and we have to accept that talented individuals were an important part of the story. But it is also true that the work of these individuals on its own would not have brought the benefits that came from the development of penicillin. If Florey and Chain had not become interested in Fleming's work, things might have happened much more slowly. If the world had not gone to war in 1939, then governments would not have poured money into mass producing penicillin. Just to confuse things even more, you might like to know that Chain said that even without Fleming, he and Florey would still have done their work. It would just have taken longer.

Stage 1 1928

Alexander Fleming discovered the penicillin mould. He was unable to produce pure penicillin from the mould. He published a report of his work but did no more.

Stage 2 1938–41

A team of researchers at Oxford University, led by Howard Florey and Ernst Chain, developed a method of making pure penicillin. They could not make large amounts however.

Stage 3 1941–4

In 1941 the USA entered the Second World War. The US government funded research into methods of making large quantities of penicillin. By 1944 enough penicillin was available for Allied soldiers.

**Stages in the penicillin story.** ▶

## The Fleming 'myth'

In August 1942 a friend of Alexander Fleming's lay dying in St Mary's Hospital. Fleming contacted Florey in Oxford and asked for some penicillin to treat his friend. Florey immediately obliged and the patient made a rapid recovery. The story appeared in *The Times* and, on 30 August 1942, Almroth Wright wrote a letter to the newspaper saying that Fleming was the person responsible for the drug. People began to believe that the development of penicillin was due entirely to Fleming. Even though Florey and Chain were awarded the Nobel Prize, along with Fleming in 1945, their part in this incredible medical breakthrough was played down.

## Source T

▲ This stained glass window, showing Alexander Fleming at work in his laboratory, was installed in St James' Church, Paddington, London. The church is very close to St Mary's Hospital, where Fleming had worked for 49 years.

## Source U

**Sir** In your article on penicillin yesterday you refrained from putting the laurel wreath for this discovery around anyone's brow. I would supplement your article by pointing out that it should be decreed to Professor Alexander Fleming of this laboratory. For he is the discoverer of penicillin and also the author of the original suggestion that this substance might ... have important applications in medicine.

▲ Extract from the letter written to *The Times* by Sir Almroth Wright. It was published on 30 August 1942.

## Source V

There has been a lot of most undesirable publicity in the newspapers and press about penicillin. The whole subject is presented as having been foreseen and worked out by Fleming. This steady propaganda seems to have its effect even on scientific people, in that several have now said to us, 'But I thought you had done something on penicillin too'.

▲ Extract from a letter written by Howard Florey to Sir Henry Dale in December 1942. Dale was the President of the Royal Society, a body concerned with the advancement of science and medicine.

# QUESTIONS

1  a  What is the Fleming 'myth'?

   b  How did it come into existence?

   c  Who do you think deserves the credit for penicillin: Fleming or Florey and Chain? Give reasons for your answer.

2  Would penicillin have been discovered even if Fleming, Florey and Chain had not lived? Explain your answer.

3  If you knew that for many years before 1900 mould from fungus had been used by people in numerous parts of the world to treat wounds, would you say that the work of Fleming, Florey and Chain was not really a breakthrough in the history of medicine? Explain your answer.

## Antibiotics

When the Second World War ended in 1945, the companies producing penicillin for the military were able to mass produce it for the public at large. The first **antibiotics** had been born.

Since 1945 drug companies have invested millions of pounds into research. They know that if they find drugs that are able to cure or prevent illness there are huge profits to be made. As a result of research hundreds of different types of antibiotics now exist. Although penicillin is still the most widely used, other antibiotics have proved more effective against certain diseases. For example streptomycin, discovered in 1944, is particularly effective in dealing with tuberculosis. Some people have proved to be allergic to penicillin and instead can now take other antibiotics, such as tetracycline or mitomycin.

## Why has illness not been ended?

As drug companies have spent more and more on research, so increasingly effective drugs have been developed. We now have vaccines which can prevent most diseases and drugs which can control irregular heartbeat or even help the heart to pump blood through damaged arteries. But the story is not one of complete success. Sometimes our new 'wonder drugs' turn out to be less effective than we would like.

## Thalidomide

In the early 1960s a new drug, **Thalidomide**, was introduced to help women who were suffering from morning sickness during pregnancy. The drug proved effective, but it had not been tested thoroughly enough. What the makers did not realise was that the drug actually caused harm to the foetus. As a result of the mothers taking thalidomide a number of children were born with severely deformed limbs. Later it was discovered that the effects of thalidomide could be passed on from generation to generation. The drug companies were forced to pay millions of pounds in compensation. Following this, in 1964 the British government set up the Committee on Safety of Drugs to screen all developed drugs.

## Source W

### £485,000 DAMAGES FOR 28 THALIDOMIDE CHILDREN

Agreed damages totalling £485,528 were awarded in the High Court yesterday to 28 deformed children who were affected by the drug thalidomide.

Seeking approval for the settlements, Mr Desmond Ackner, the children's lawyer, revealed that negotiations were taking place to provide for 300 other children thought to have been deformed by thalidomide.

Discussions were being held with the Distillers Company (Biochemicals) Ltd. to set up a trust. This would save the 'years of time' it would take to deal with all the children on an individual basis.

▲ An article from the *Daily Telegraph*, July 1970.

## Superbugs

One of the most worrying developments in medicine since the introduction of antibiotics has been the demand from busy people to take antibiotics as an instant cure for their illnesses. This has resulted in the overuse of antibiotics with the result that certain bacteria are beginning to develop resistance to their effects. Consequently people have to be given stronger antibiotics when they are ill, and this means bacteria are beginning to develop immunity to these stronger antibiotics.

A member of the US Department of Health recently said:

*'The concern is that we may run out of weapons to deal with severe infections. When used properly, antibiotics save lives. But when used incorrectly bacteria can form defences, mutate, and ultimately outwit the medicine and survive.'*

Scientists have begun to call bacteria which are resistant to antibiotics 'superbugs'.

## Source X

Like characters in a bad horror movie we had our backs turned when bacteria we thought we'd beaten, rose up with new powers and began to fight back. Within just a few years of the introduction of antibiotics, a troubling pattern emerged. Bacteria frequently treated with the same antibiotic would eventually develop resistance to the drug. Another antibiotic would have to be used until the bug learned to resist that drug too.

Hospitals are particularly fertile breeding grounds for these superbugs. It is estimated than more than two million Americans acquire infections in hospital each year and between 60,000 and 80,000 of them die as a result.

▲ A recent report on the power of superbugs in the USA.

## AIDS

**AIDS** (Acquired Immune Deficiency Syndrome) is a new disease for which no cure has yet been found. It first came to the attention of US doctors in 1981 when they realised that young gay men were dying in large numbers from unrecognised conditions involving the breakdown of the body's immune system.

By 1983 the HIV virus had been discovered to be the cause. No one really knows where the disease has come from and various theories have been put forward. One suggestion is that it had previously been restricted to small areas of African rain forest, but increased communication led to it being spread across the world. Whatever the origin of the disease, it had, up to the end of 2001, killed almost 25 million people.

|  | Adults (millions) | Children under 15 (millions) |
|---|---|---|
| No. of people living with AIDS | 37.2 | 2.7 |
| AIDS deaths up to 2001 | 17.5 | 4.3 |
| AIDS deaths in 2001 | 2.4 | 0.6 |
| No. of children orphaned by AIDS |  | 13.2 million |

| The proportion of adults living with AIDS in 2001 | |
|---|---|
| Africa, south of the Sahara | 8.4% |
| Caribbean | 2.2% |
| North America | 0.6% |
| South and South East Asia | 0.6% |
| South America | 0.5% |
| Western Europe | 0.3% |

## Source Y

AIDS has driven a coach and horses through the idea that disease is being conquered. We quickly recognised it and put our best brains to work on it. We made it a household word. All in vain. It spread through Africa and the Americas, crossed the seas to Europe and Asia and is now the leading cause of death in young adults in many parts of the world.

▲ Matt Ridley, in his book *Disease*, written in the USA in 1997.

### Tuberculosis

It isn't just new diseases which are causing problems. We thought we had conquered tuberculosis, but now it too is beginning to show signs of resistance to antibiotics. Between 1985 and 1991 tuberculosis increased by 12 per cent in the USA, 30 per cent in Europe and a massive 300 per cent in parts of Africa. The disease kills more than three million people each year, 95 per cent of them in the less economically-developed world.

### Genetic engineering – hope for the future?

With technological advances, in particular more powerful microscopes, scientists have been able to study human cells and the genes and chromosomes within them. This has allowed them to develop means of 'genetic engineering' where the genetic material within a person is altered by destroying specific damaged or diseased cells. Such a practice is still in its early years, but has already proved valuable in the treatment of cancers, blood, liver and lung disorders. Some medical experts believe that the time will come when spare 'body parts' could be cloned to replace damaged or diseased organs. Perhaps in the future we will be able to transplant test-tube grown parts into our own bodies.

## QUESTIONS

1  What lessons can we learn about medicine from:

   a  the Thalidomide affair
   b  superbugs
   c  AIDS?

## SUMMARY

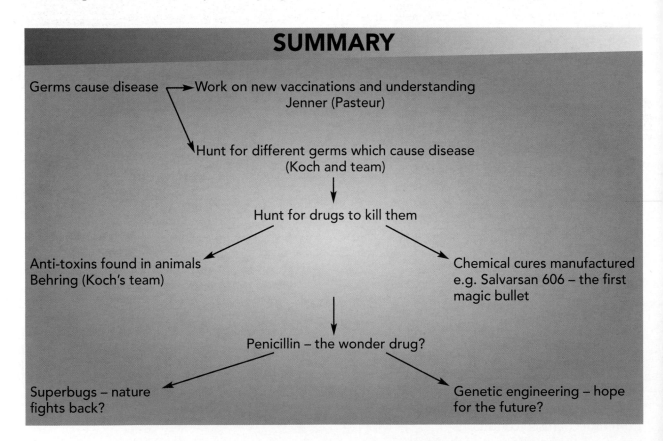

Germs cause disease → Work on new vaccinations and understanding Jenner (Pasteur)

Hunt for different germs which cause disease (Koch and team)

Hunt for drugs to kill them

Anti-toxins found in animals Behring (Koch's team)

Chemical cures manufactured e.g. Salvarsan 606 – the first magic bullet

Penicillin – the wonder drug?

Superbugs – nature fights back?

Genetic engineering – hope for the future?

## Source 1

▲ Pasteur and his team. Dr Emile Roux, his main assistant, is seated on his right. Albert Calmette who, together with Camille Guerin, discovered a vaccine against TB in 1906, is seated on the far right of Pasteur.

## Source 2

Pasteur was a small man capable of inspiring devotion in others. He also had aggressive manners which could make people who were equally as clever both bitter and turn them into enemies. One of his strongest motivations was to show how much more clever he was by destroying their arguments entirely.
**Nationalism** was a powerful force in his life. He wanted to work for the glory of France. He worshipped the French Emperor, Napoleon III. When France and Prussia (part of Germany) went to war in 1870, his hatred of the Germans was intense. Personal ambition was very important to him. He wanted to be famous.

▲ This opinion of Pasteur was written by Robert Reid in *Microbes and Men*, 1974.

## Source 3

At the International Conference of Hygiene in Geneva, 1882, Koch left Pasteur in no doubt that he believed that Pasteur had contributed nothing new to science. Pasteur lost his temper and years of hatred came out. Yet Pasteur's work had been the great idea, Koch's scientific skill had made its application possible.

▲ Robert Reid's analysis of the conflict between Pasteur and Koch in *Microbes and Men*, 1974.

## Source 4

I am very satisfied with the success of the experiments with the rabid dogs. You must keep a careful check on the dogs and a daily written record of what happens to them, making absolutely certain whether they become ill or not, or if they should be cured.

▲ From a letter written to Eurgene Viala by Louis Pasteur, 6 September 1883. Viala was a member of Pasteur's team and was assisting in the research on the rabies vaccine.

## Source 5

▲ Louis Pasteur vaccinating a sheep against anthrax in 1881.

1 Study Sources 1, 3 and 4.

   a What factors can you find in these sources that enabled Pasteur to make his discoveries?

   b What other factors also contributed to Pasteur's achievements?

   c Which of the factors that helped Pasteur to make his discoveries do you think was the most important? Explain your answer.

   d Can you find any evidence in the sources to explain why Pasteur faced opposition? Explain your answer.

2 Study Source 2. 'This is just a boring "mugshot" of some men in a room. It does not help us understand anything about Pasteur.' Explain how far you agree with this statement.

3 Study Source 5.

   a What could a historian studying the history of medicine learn from this source?

   b Do you think that this drawing gives a reliable impression of how Pasteur carried out his work? Explain your answer.

4 There were many important people working in medicine in the 19th century. Three examples are:

   ● Pasteur
   ● Ehrlich
   ● Koch.

   Which of these three do you think made the most important contribution? Explain your answer.

# CHAPTER 12

# THE REVOLUTION IN SURGERY

## 12.1 Anaesthetics conquer pain

### Problem of pain

Surgeons had long had to face the problems of pain, infection and bleeding. This was still true in the early-19th century. There were no effective anaesthetics. Surgeons gave their patients drugs like **opium** and mandrake, or tried to get them drunk. A few surgeons used 'mesmerism' (hypnosis), hoping the patient would ignore the pain. Surgery had to be quick. Deep internal operations were out of the question. Most surgery was limited to removing growths or amputating limbs. Even so, many patients died from the trauma of the excruciating pain.

During the late-18th century the science of chemistry had made some progress. In 1772 Joseph Priestley, an English chemist, discovered that oxygen was a gas. Other chemists were also investigating the properties of different substances. In 1799 Humphrey Davy (1778–1829) discovered pain could be relieved by inhaling nitrous oxide ('laughing gas'). He wrote a pamphlet saying that nitrous oxide might be successfully used as an anaesthetic by surgeons. The medical profession, however, ignored his suggestion.

**Anaesthetics** are drugs given to a patient to make surgery pain free.

There are two types:

**General anaesthetics** – these are drugs which are usually inhaled and render the patient unconscious.

**Local anaesthetics** – these are usually injected and have the effect of numbing one particular part of the body such as a tooth. They do not make the patient unconscious.

## Source A

◄ A cartoon drawn by Thomas Rowlandson, showing an operation in 1793. The list of doctors' names on the wall shows that the cartoonist saw doctors as more concerned with money than with caring for their patients.

## Source B

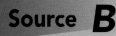

A patient preparing for an operation was like a condemned criminal preparing for an execution.

▲ From a letter written to James Simpson in 1848, by a man who had undergone surgery before effective anaesthetics.

## Early successes

During the early-1840s a number of experiments were made to find an effective anaesthetic. In 1842 the American doctor, Crawford Long, found that ether was a useful anaesthetic, but did not publicly announce his discovery.

On 10 December 1845 an American dentist, Horace Wells, saw people inhaling nitrous oxide at a fair. He noticed that they could injure themselves, but felt no pain. The next day, Wells had a tooth painlessly taken out after inhaling the gas. He tried to demonstrate painless tooth extraction to some medical students at a Hospital in Boston, USA. What he did not know was that some people are not affected by nitrous oxide. Wells' volunteer yelled as the tooth was taken out. The students left shouting 'Humbug! Humbug!'

On 16 October 1846 William Thomas Green Morton (1819–68) persuaded John Warren, the head surgeon at the Boston Hospital, to carry out an operation in public using ether as an anaesthetic. The patient, Gilbert Abbott, was given ether through an inhaler by Morton. Warren proceeded to remove a tumour painlessly from his neck. Warren turned to his audience and announced: 'Gentlemen, this is no humbug!'

News of Warren's success spread quickly to Europe. By 18 October, a Dr Bigelow, who had seen the operation, had published an article on it. On 3 December a steamship carried a letter from Bigelow to a Dr Boot in London. By 19 December Dr Boot had extracted a tooth using ether – and had written an article about it. On 21 December the surgeon, Robert Liston, successfully amputated the leg of Frederick Churchill (a butler) using ether as an anaesthetic. Liston removed the leg in 26 seconds! With the leg already on the floor, Churchill raised his head and asked Liston when he was going to begin the operation.

## Source C

▲ Warren's operation on Gilbert Abbott, 16 October 1846, painted by Robert Hinckley in 1882.

## Source D

This Yankee dodge, gentlemen, beats mesmerism hollow!

▲ A remark made by Robert Liston to the audience after his public operation on Frederick Churchill at the University College Hospital, London.

# QUESTIONS

1 What problems of surgery are shown in Source A?

2 Make out a chart, like the one below, to record the times when experiments were made with anaesthetics.

| Date | Event | Person(s) involved |
|------|-------|--------------------|
|      |       |                    |

3 Source C is a painting completed after the event. Is it a reliable source of evidence for a historian? Explain your answer.

4 Study Source D. What do you think Liston meant?

## James Simpson and chloroform

James Young Simpson (1811–70), Professor of Midwifery at Edinburgh University, wanted to find something which relieved pain during childbirth. He disliked ether because it was inflammable, had a pungent smell and, when inhaled, irritated the lungs making the patient cough. He began to test the effects of different chemicals. On 4 November 1847 Simpson and two other doctors discovered the effects of chloroform (see Source E). Simpson found chloroform easier to administer than ether. Less of it was needed and it appeared to take effect more quickly. By the end of November he had given chloroform to more than 50 patients and he declared himself pleased with the outcome.

## Opposition to anaesthetics

These anaesthetics meant painless operations, but they were not welcomed by everyone.

- Some people worried that surgeons were too inexperienced. They were unsure as to the correct amount to give or of any side effects they could have. There were even instances of explosions in operating theatres caused by the use of ether. Their fears appeared to be realized when, in 1848, Hannah Green, aged fifteen, died from an overdose of chloroform. Deaths also occurred from the overuse of ether.
- Members of the Calvinist Church in Scotland were outraged at the use of chloroform in childbirth. They pointed to the Book of Genesis where God says to Eve: 'In sorrow shalt thou bring forth children.' In other words, God intended women to bear pain when giving birth.
- Some people were worried that anaesthetics placed the patient under the total control of the surgeons. What if they did something against the patient's will?
- In the army some officers regarded the use of anaesthetics as 'soft'. In 1854 John Hall, Chief of Medical Staff in the Crimea, told his team of doctors: 'A good hand on the knife is stimulating. It is much better to hear a fellow shouting with all his might than to see him sink quietly into his grave.'

## Source E

Late one evening Dr Simpson with his two friends and assistants, sat down to their somewhat hazardous work in Dr Simpson's dining room. Having sniffed several substances, but without much effect, it occurred to Dr Simpson to try a material which he had regarded as likely to be of no use whatever; that happened to be a small bottle of chloroform. It was searched for and recovered from beneath a heap of waste paper. [They inhaled the chloroform and passed out.] On awakening Dr Simpson's first thought was, 'This is far stronger and better than ether.'

▲ From H. L. Gordon, *Sir James Young Simpson and Chloroform*, 1897.

## Source F

▲ A 19th century drawing showing the effect of inhaling chloroform on Simpson and his assistants.

## The royal seal of approval!

Some of this opposition disappeared when, on 7 April 1853, Queen Victoria was given chloroform during the birth of her eighth child, Prince Leopold. The anaesthetist was Dr John Snow, later to do vital research into cholera. The Queen wrote in her journal that chloroform was 'soothing, quietening and delightful beyond measure.' Chloroform became socially more acceptable as a result of the Queen's experience. It became the most popular anaesthetic until about 1900, when it was realized that it could damage the liver. Surgeons then returned to using ether.

## Anaesthetics from the late-19th century to the present day

Even though anaesthetics came to be accepted, there were still problems in using them. Massive amounts were often needed, not to prevent pain, but to relax the muscles. Patients became saturated and slept for hours, even days. Recovery was slow and there were frequent complications.

From the end of the 19th century, anaesthetists became specialists. New substances were discovered and put into use. In 1884 cocaine was first used as a local anaesthetic, numbing one part of the body while the patient remained conscious. In Germany, in 1905, novocaine was proved to be more effective than cocaine. In 1942 curare, a South American poison, was first used as a muscle relaxant during operations; it remains in use today. A skilled anaesthetist is now a crucial member of the surgical team, responsible for monitoring the patient's well-being during operations.

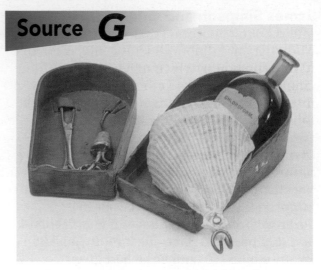

▲ A chloroform inhaler from 1879. It consists of a cotton facemask on to which the chloroform was poured.

## QUESTIONS

1  Why did Simpson dislike ether?

2  Does Source E show that chance played a part in the discovery of chloroform?

3  What other factors enabled Simpson to make his discovery?

4  a  Why was there such fierce opposition to anaesthetics?

   b  How was this opposition overcome?

Source **H**

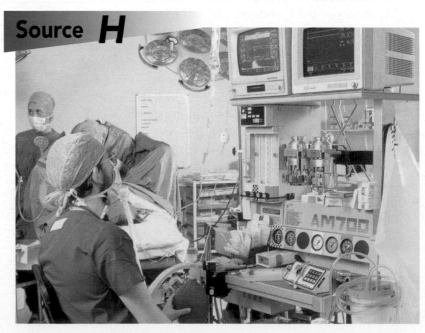

▶ Modern anaesthetists at work. Anaesthetists now monitor heart beat, blood pressure, breathing patterns and brain waves using high-technology equipment.

## The problem of infection

The period between the first use of ether as an anaesthetic in 1846 and about 1870 has been called the 'black period' of surgery. The removal of pain made surgeons over confident and they performed many operations that they would not have attempted before anaesthetics. Operations, however, were still carried out in unhygienic conditions. Surgeons wore their everyday clothes when operating and instruments were not sterilized between operations. Before Pasteur proved the germ theory the need for cleanliness was not understood. As a result, many patients died from the infections that developed after the operation.

## Ignaz Semmelweiss

Semmelweiss was a young Hungarian doctor working in Vienna in the 1840s. He was worried about the high death rate of women from puerperal fever, an infection which set in after childbirth. Some doctors believed this was spread by miasmas present in the air of hospital wards. In 1847 Semmelweiss suggested that the doctors themselves might be spreading the infection by examining patients immediately after dissecting the dead bodies of victims of the disease. He ordered the doctors to wash their hands in a solution of chloride of lime before examining patients. This was unpleasant and many doctors resented it. But the death rate from puerperal fever in these wards fell dramatically. Other doctors did not accept Semmelweiss' method. The high death rates continued in most places.

## Joseph Lister and antiseptics

The breakthrough in preventing infection was made by Joseph Lister. He had read of Pasteur's research and he realized that the infections that were killing his patients were caused by germs. To kill any germs that were present he decided to use carbolic acid, a disinfectant that was used to combat the smell at sewage works. He knew that the smell of rotting sewage and the operating theatre were similar. First he used bandages soaked in the acid, then he developed his technique to include a spray that drenched the air, the surgeon's hands, the instruments and the patient. This was unpleasant for surgeons but the results were remarkable. Mortality plummeted and when Lister died in 1912, ten times as many operations were being performed as there had been in 1867. Surgeons were able, for the first time, to operate without fear of infection killing the patient. The combination of anaesthetics and antiseptics meant that surgery was now much safer.

### JOSEPH LISTER
#### (1828–1912)

Joseph Lister came from a well off family in Essex. By the time he was 33, he was Professor of Surgery at Glasgow University. Although, at first, many doctors opposed his ideas, Lister was recognized for making one of the greatest advances ever in surgery.

The figures below come from his records of amputations.

| Date | No. of patients | % died |
|---|---|---|
| 1864–6 (no antiseptics) | 35 | 46% |
| 1867–70 (antiseptics) | 40 | 15% |

## Source 1

Lister's creativity was a simple process. Chance had not helped in his discovery. He had read of the germ theory of disease and had applied it. The only significant piece of luck involved was the sweeping effects of the consequences. Millions of lives were saved by the new principle of **antisepsis** [the use of antiseptics to kill germs] and what followed it. The frightful spectre which had haunted operating theatres had at last been shown to have an organic cause, and Lister had shown how to defeat it.

▲ Robert Reid, *Microbes and Men*, 1974.

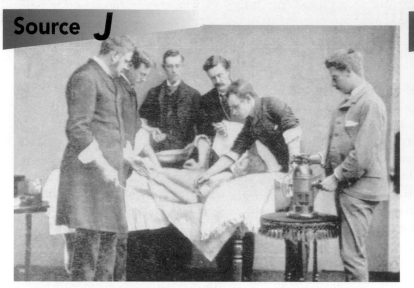

▲ An antiseptic operation in Aberdeen in the 1880s. Lister's steam carbolic spray is being used.

Despite the [support] of statistical evidence, Lister's method met with interference and even violent opposition … Fully twenty years of patient trial, improvement, demonstration and education were needed before British surgeons were won over to the idea, and not before many senior members of the profession had been replaced by a younger generation.

▲ Leo M. Zimmermann and Ilza Veith, *Great Ideas in the History of Surgery*, 1961.

### From antiseptic to aseptic surgery

Antiseptic surgery had its drawbacks, not least being the discomfort felt by surgeons and nurses whose skin was burnt by the carbolic acid and lungs irritated by the spray. Rather than trying to fight germs, surgeons in Germany developed techniques for keeping them away. This is known as **asepsis** and aseptic surgery quickly became the normal procedure in the operating theatre. The idea of scrupulous cleanliness originated with Professor Neuber and was developed by Ernst Bergmann. Surgeons' hands, clothes and instruments were all sterilized. A chamber was used to pass superheated steam over the instruments, thus killing the germs without the need for disinfecting chemicals.

The 'father' of American surgery, William S. Halsted, introduced a further innovation. In 1889 his nurse, Caroline Hampton, complained that antiseptic chemicals were harming her hands. Halsted asked the Goodyear Rubber Company to make some gloves. He had a particular interest as he was to marry Nurse Hampton in 1890. Halsted realized that the gloves were protecting the patient as well as the nurse. He followed this by introducing caps, masks and gowns for surgery. Halsted also investigated cocaine as

▲ Halsted in the operating theatre at the Johns Hopkins Medical School, Baltimore, USA. He operated and taught his students at the same time.

an anaesthetic but became a drug addict, taking both cocaine and morphine.

Today instruments are pre-packed in sterile containers. The air is sterilized before it enters the operating theatre. Some operations, especially on babies or for joint replacement, take place in sterile 'tents' to ensure that there is no risk of infection.

## Plastic surgery

Grafting skin to repair damaged features was practised in ancient India and during the Renaissance but infection was a major problem. The development of new weapons in the 20th century meant that the number and type of facial and skin wounds increased. In Britain, Harold Gillies set up a unit to treat horrific wounds inflicted during the First World War. He was the first plastic surgeon to consider the patient's appearance. Gillies' assistant was a New Zealander, Archibald McIndoe. In the Second World War, McIndoe set up a unit at East Grinstead in Sussex where he treated over 4000 patients, mostly airmen, whose faces and hands were disfigured by blazing petrol. His patients, known as 'guinea pigs', were helped by developments in drugs like sulphonamides and penicillin that helped prevent infection. Plastic surgery has become a vital branch of surgery, bringing better quality of life to people whose lives would otherwise be shattered by injury or birth defects.

**Source** *M*

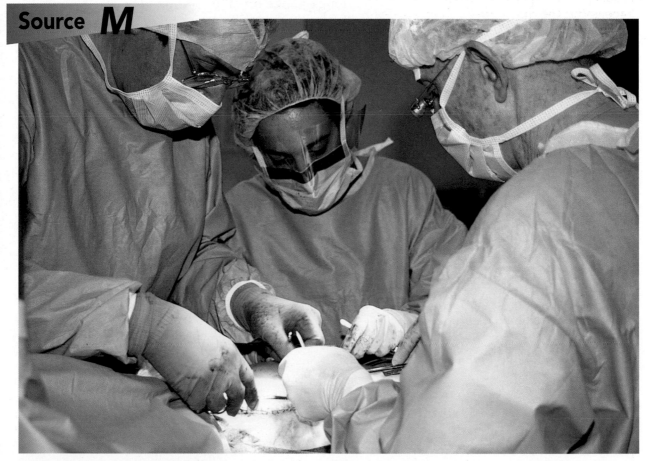

▲ **A modern plastic surgery operation. The patient is undergoing reconstruction of one of her breasts following treatment for breast cancer.**

# ARCHIBALD MCINDOE
## 'The face-builder'

Born: Dunedin, New Zealand 1900.

Career: Studied medicine at Otago, the Mayo Clinic and St Bartholomew's Hospital in London. After the First World War he worked with the British surgeon, Harold Gillies in treating patients who had suffered disfigurement as a result of wounds received in the war.

During the Second World War, McIndoe ran a special plastic surgery unit at East Grinstead in England. He specialised in plastic surgery on the faces and limbs of airmen who had suffered burns when their planes had been shot down. A good example of this can be seen in a recent obituary of an ex-RAF pilot published in June 2002. The obituary describes how 'the pilot's fuel tank caught fire, spilling fuel over the cockpit and the pilot himself. He was taken to East Grinstead, where the pioneering surgeon Sir Archibald McIndoe, rebuilt his hands and carried out skin grafts.

Honours won: knighted in 1947 (became Sir Archibald McIndoe).

Died 1960. As a symbol of gratitude his ashes were buried in the RAF church in London.

## High technology surgery

Surgeons could often benefit from the rapid development of science and technology in the late 19th and 20th centuries. The increasing use of electricity meant that many machines could be developed to assist surgery. Plastics and steel enabled artificial joints to be made for replacement surgery.

- In 1895 Wilhelm Röntgen, professor of physics at the University of Würzburg, discovered X-rays. These enabled surgeons to look at the inside of a patient without making any incision.
- Marie and Pierre Curie discovered a new element, radium, in 1898. This eventually led to improved treatment for cancer.
- In 1903 the first electrocardiograph was developed by Willem Einthoven. Eventually it enabled surgeons to monitor the heartbeat effectively.
- The first artificial kidney machine was developed in 1943 by the Dutch surgeon, Willem Kolff.
- The first successful operation with a heart-lung machine, which enabled the heart to be stopped long enough for an operation to be carried out, took place in 1953.
- Efficient microscopes for surgeons to use when operating were developed in the 1960s. Along with fine **sutures** and needles, they made it possible for doctors to join microscopic nerves and blood vessels and even to reattach severed limbs. One strange result of the development of microsurgery was the reintroduction of leeches in the 1980s because they are efficient in keeping blood flowing in an affected limb.

- The development of **fibre optics** has meant that it is now possible to examine the inside of a patient's body and to operate without having to make a large wound.
- Miniature cameras called endoscopes have been developed which can be inserted into the body through the mouth or the bowels, via the rectum. As surgeons can see 'from the inside', they do not need to make large incisions.
- This 'keyhole surgery' means that patients can have a local, rather than a general anaesthetic. Their body suffers less shock and recovery is much quicker.

## Heart surgery

Before the Second World War, surgery on the heart was dangerous and rarely carried out. When surgeons opened the chest, the patient's lungs collapsed and when the heart was touched, it stopped. It was thought that nothing could be done about this.

The Second World War provided the stimulus for further research as some soldiers had bullets and fragments of shrapnel lodged in their hearts. A US army surgeon, Dwight Harken, had the courage to try to save them. He cut into the beating heart and used his finger to remove the fragments. The problem for the patients who needed open heart surgery to correct defects was that the blood supply needed to be cut off when the heart was opened. After four minutes, this would cause brain damage. A Canadian surgeon, Bill Biggelow, came up with the idea of lowering the patient's body temperature to gain more time. Nevertheless the problem remained.

▼ A surgeon using an endoscope to look inside the patient. It is inserted through a small incision near the patient's navel.

**Source N**

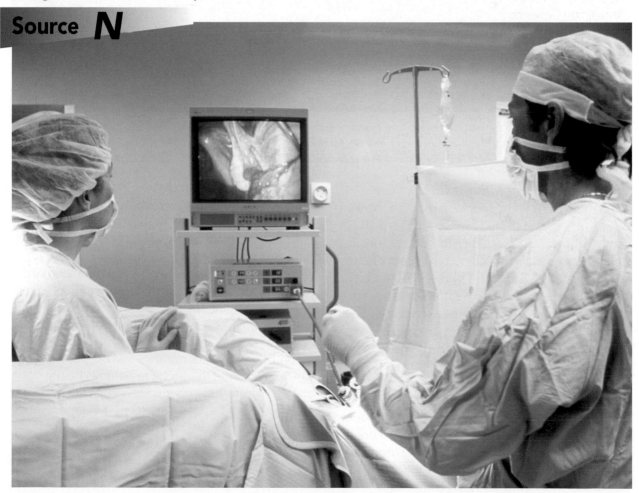

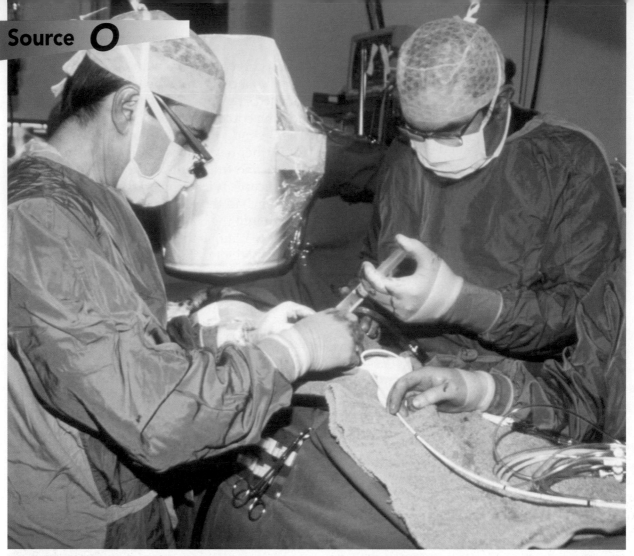

▲ Surgeons attaching a patient to a heart-lung machine during heart valve surgery. This machine takes over the circulation of the patient's blood and provides oxygen for the blood. Before the invention of this machine, surgeons could not operate on the heart for more than a few minutes.

At the University of Minnesota, Norman Shumway led a team specializing in pioneering heart surgery but there was sometimes a 50 per cent death rate. In 1960 the Methodist Hospital in Houston, Texas, became the centre for heart surgery under Michael de Blakey. He worked at immense speed and used knitted Dacron, an artificial fibre, to replace diseased arteries. The problem of transplanting a replacement heart remained. Tissue rejection made it seem impossible. However, research continued despite the shortage of human hearts. In 1967 Norman Shumway announced that he was ready to try a human heart transplant. In New York, Dr Adrian Kantrowitz prepared to operate on a baby on 3 December. That same morning he heard that Christiaan Barnard had performed the world's first human heart transplant.

## Christiaan Barnard

Surgeons in the USA were disappointed, as they felt that they had done all the experimental work and Barnard had used their ideas. He denied this. Shumway and Kantrowitz carried out their operations but their patients soon died. Barnard did another transplant and his patient lived over a year-and-a-half. In Texas, Michael de Blakey and Denton Cooley also tried human transplants. Cooley was able to complete a transplant operation in twenty minutes. No one, however, could overcome the problems caused by the patient's immune system. The drugs the patients needed to get the body to accept the donor heart, left them open to infection. They always died within a relatively short time.

## CHRISTIAAN BARNARD
### Pioneering surgeon

Born: Beaufort West, South Africa 1923.

Career: Walked five miles each day to study at Cape Town University and qualified as a family doctor. In the late 1950s he went to the USA to study heart treatment at the University of Minnesota.

In 1967 he transplanted the heart of a female road accident victim into 59 year-old Louis Washkansky. Although Washkansky died 18 days later, Barnard had shown that the operation was possible. He became world-famous and was invited to meet the Pope in Rome and the US President Johnson in Washington. He was surprised by the publicity. As he said 'I didn't even inform the hospital superintendent what we were doing'.

Died: 2001.

Enormous public expectation had been shattered. The failure rate was too high. Barnard tried to keep transplants going but did not succeed. Some saw him as the villain. Heart transplant operations ceased. Some doctors turned to experimenting with artificial hearts and, in 1982, Barney Clarke was given a plastic heart in Salt Lake City, USA. He died three weeks later.

The solution arrived by chance. In 1974 a researcher in Norway looking for new drug substances in soil samples came across the drug cyclosporin. It was found it controlled tissue rejection but did not eliminate all resistance to disease. Cyclosporin had a more dramatic effect on heart transplant surgery than the skills of Barnard and Cooley combined because it meant that transplants were possible again. By 1987, 90 per cent of patients lived more than two years. Heart transplants are now routine. Surgery, drugs, patient care and the control of rejection all interlink to give success.

## Source P

Tiny tubes, wires, balloons, coils, glue, plastic particles – these sound like pieces of a child's construction kit, not the tools of a rapidly growing branch of medicine. But the chances are that soon your doctor will be threading a few of those tools into your blood vessels or possibly going right through the skin into one of your organs. The doctor will be using the tools to treat you, not just to look to see what's there. And the treatment will be done with the constant guidance of powerful imaging machines, like ultra scanners, X-ray and computerised tomography.

▲ **A US doctor writing on how high-tech surgery will soon be so straightforward that doctors will be able to use it, as well as surgeons in hospitals.**

## Source Q

One hundred and fifty years ago, patients would only lie on the operating table in desperation when they were tortured by agony from their gangrenous leg or stones in the bladder. Now with modern anaesthesia, with antiseptics, with blood transfusion, with antibiotics – the modern miracles of surgery – nothing can escape. Everything, from the brain to bunions, is available for the surgeon's healing knife.

▲ **A comment made by Professor Harold Ellis of Westminster Hospital to a group of medical students in the BBC television programme, *The Courage to Fail*, in 1987.**

Administrators decided we were spending too much. They had the enormous stupidity to suggest that, if we kept patients out, we could work within budget. I said, 'No problem. We've got a shot gun. I'll load it. You fire it, because that's what you're planning. Now, out.'

▲ **Denis Melrose, a leading British heart surgeon, describing a difficulty he faced in the 1960s.**

## SUMMARY

▶ The combination of anaesthetics and antiseptics, developed by Joseph Lister, meant that surgery became much safer after 1870.

▶ Aseptic surgery, when no germs are ever allowed to be present, soon replaced antiseptic surgery.

▶ The discovery of the different blood groups allowed safe transfusions thus reducing the risks from blood loss in surgery.

▶ Surgeons began to specialize as surgery became safer. Plastic, brain and heart surgery were developed by pioneering individuals.

▶ Developments in science and technology contributed to new techniques in medicine.

▶ The wars fought in the 20th century speeded up developments in surgery.

## The impact of high-tech surgery

The work of Christiaan Barnard and other 'pioneering surgeons' has been important in expanding the boundaries of surgery. We can now carry out operations which would only have been dreamt of 30 years ago. Transplants are now common and it is only a shortage of donors which stops them being carried out even more frequently. Some medical scientists dream of the day when we will be able to **clone** human organs ready to carry out a transplant if necessary.

Improved technology has meant that the use of lasers has become an accepted part of treatment. Lasers are used in minor operations, such as correcting eye faults, or in life-saving situations where cancers can be controlled through laser treatment. Our skill and technology has even increased to the point where we can detect problems with unborn babies and carry out corrective surgery even before the child has been born.

The wide range of surgery now available has had a major effect on the finances of hospitals and the NHS is facing great difficulties funding all the operations which could be carried out. A heart transplant is a wonderful thing for the recipient, but is so expensive that it might take funds away from other, seemingly less-important areas, such as hip replacements for the elderly. Many hospitals are forced to juggle their budgets to keep their operating theatres working. A tragic consequence of this is that surgeons sometimes have to 'prioritise' operations. There have been cases where treatment for 'self-imposed illness', perhaps as a result of smoking, has been put lower down the list of priorities than other treatment. Both surgeons and patients find this a very difficult situation to cope with (see also page 137).

## QUESTIONS

1 Study Source I (page 107), Source J (page 108) and Source O (page 112). What changes in surgery do they show?

2 a How important have individuals been in the development of surgery since 1870?
  b How has science and technology helped surgery develop since 1870?
  c What other factors have played a part in the development of surgery since 1870?

3 Some books claim that Christiaan Barnard made the most important breakthrough in the history of heart surgery. On the evidence in this chapter, do you agree?

4 Read Sources Q and R. In what way does Source R suggest that things are not as rosy as suggested in Source Q?

5 'It can't be right that some patients are deliberately refused treatment.' Explain whether you agree with this statement.

In 1850, nursing was looked upon as a lowly occupation. Nurses were generally portrayed as uneducated and slovenly and they had a reputation for heavy drinking. This image, however, was not totally fair. The conditions under which they worked were often appalling and there was no proper training available. At Kaiserwerth in Germany, however, the local pastor, Theodor Fliedner, set up a small hospital and training school in 1853. He insisted that his nurses be of 'good character'. Elizabeth Fry, famous for her attempts to reform prison conditions in London's Newgate gaol, visited Kaiserwerth in 1840. She was so impressed that on her return to England she founded Britain's first nursing school, the Institute of Nursing Sisters. During the second half of the 19th century nursing underwent a revolution and developed into a respected profession. How did this change come about?

## The Crimean War (1854–6): a tale of two women

Florence Nightingale (1820–1910) came from a wealthy middle-class family. In 1844 she told her parents that she wanted to enter nursing. Her parents naturally had a low opinion of nurses and it took Florence seven years of determined effort to persuade them to agree. She then visited Kaiserwerth, travelling on to Paris to study nursing. In 1853 she became the Superintendent at the Institution for the Care of Sick Gentlewomen in Harley Street, London which she ran very efficiently. By now she was fully committed to a career involving the training of nurses.

In March 1854 Britain, along with France and Turkey, went to war against Russia. The war was fought in the Crimea, a peninsula on the Black Sea, three thousand miles from Britain. A scandal broke when the public read the reports of William Russell, the war correspondent of *The Times* newspaper. He told of chaotic conditions in the Barrack Hospital in Scutari near Constantinople. Wounded British troops were being kept in overcrowded and filthy conditions. There were no nursing staff, no bandages and men were dying in agony.

## Nightingale's work at Scutari

The Secretary of War, Sidney Herbert, who was a friend of the Nightingale family, wrote to ask Florence if she would 'go and superintend the whole thing'. She agreed to Herbert's request and, in the autumn of 1854, departed for Scutari in Turkey with a team of 38 nurses whom she had personally selected. When they arrived in Scutari, they were not warmly welcomed by the army doctors who felt that female nurses were 'unfavourable to military discipline and to the recovery of the patients'. Despite this undercurrent of hostility, Nightingale made sure that the wards were clean, the patients well fed, the sanitation and water supply improved and that supplies were plentiful. By early 1856 the death rate in the hospital had fallen from 42 per cent to 2 per cent.

## Source S

▲ This illustration shows how nurses were often portrayed in the 19th century – old and unattractive and possibly drunk.

## Source T

She was a woman of iron will and imposed her ideas of nursing and medical care on those in authority and on her nurses. She had friends in the high place of the Cabinet. Through an endless stream of letters … she determined to improve nursing education and care … It can only be said that she succeeded mightily, in that every nurse, every patient, every hospital design, the organization of medical and nursing services everywhere, owe something to her … spirit.

▲ Philip Rhodes, *An Outline History of Medicine*, 1985.

## Source U

She was a wonderful woman ... All the men ... would seek her advice and use her herbal medicines, in preference to reporting themselves to their own doctors ... Her never failing presence among the wounded after a battle and assisting them made her loved by the rank and file of the whole army.

▲ Memories of Mary Seacole by a British soldier who fought in the Crimean War.

## The work of Mary Seacole

Mary Jane Seacole (1805–81) was born in Kingston, Jamaica. Her mother ran a boarding house for invalid soldiers where Mary helped to care for the patients. In 1854 she went to England and told the War Office she was willing to go to the Crimea as a nurse. She was rejected and felt that it was because her 'blood flowed beneath a somewhat duskier skin than theirs'. In other words she was a victim of Victorian racism.

Not to be outdone, she made her own way to the Crimea and at her own expense. She set up a medical store and hostel near Balaclava, where soldiers could obtain medicines. She also tended the wounded on the battlefield and became known to the troops as 'Mother Seacole'. She met Florence Nightingale on several occasions but was not invited to join her team of nurses.

## Seacole's fortunes after the Crimean War

In 1856 Mary Seacole returned to England but not to a heroine's welcome. She went bankrupt and received a deal of sympathy from the English press, notably *The Times* and *Punch* magazine. A four day festival of music was organized for her benefit in 1857, but it raised only £233. In the same year, Mary published her lifestory (see Source Y) in an effort to raise money. Although she was quite well-off when she died, no one in the medical world had bothered to make use of her nursing skills since the end of the Crimean War.

## Source V

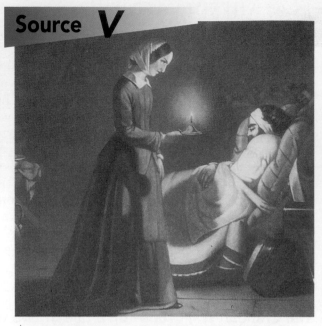

▲ A legend grew up around Florence Nightingale. She became known as 'the lady with the lamp' and 'an angel of mercy'. She was said to tour the wards at night making sure the patients were comfortable. This picture was painted by Tomkins in 1855.

## Source W

▲ A rare portrait of Mary Seacole. It appears on the title page of her autobiography, *The Wonderful Adventures of Mrs Seacole*, published in 1857.

▲ **A ward in the military hospital at Scutari, after it had been cleaned and reorganized by Nightingale nurses.**

## Nursing becomes a profession

Florence Nightingale returned to England and immediately won huge public acclaim. *The Times*, however, commented: 'While the benevolent deeds of Florence Nightingale are being handed down to posterity … are the human actions of Mrs Seacole to be entirely forgotten?' (24 November 1856). Nightingale had high hopes that her success in the Crimea would enable her to establish nursing as a respected profession. In 1859 she published a book called *Notes on Nursing* which described her methods. It stressed the importance of professionalism and ward hygiene and became the standard text for trainee nurses.

A public fund was opened to enable Nightingale to develop the training of nurses. It raised £44,000 and the money was used to start up the Nightingale School of Nursing at St Thomas's Hospital in London. It was here that the standards were laid down for the training of nurses. Trainees had to be disciplined and willing to work hard. They served a one-year probationary period and then trained for a further two years in order to qualify. Other training schools followed her example and, by 1900, there were 64,000 trained nurses in Britain.

In 1919 the Registration of Nurses Act was passed which laid down the qualifications needed to enter nursing. Today men also choose nursing as a career and it remains a highly respected profession.

## QUESTIONS

1 What were the personal qualities of Florence Nightingale and Mary Seacole?

2 What contribution did each woman make to the nursing of troops during the Crimean War?

3 Was the presence of both women welcomed by the British army? Explain your answer.

4 Which woman is more important in the development of nursing as a profession? Give reasons for your answer.

5 Was a strong personality the only factor in Nightingale's success? Explain your answer.

In the mid-19th century women were not allowed to enter the universities. It was impossible, therefore, for them to obtain a degree in medicine and become practising doctors. In 1849 Elizabeth Blackwell, an American woman born in Britain, was awarded a medical degree by a New York college. In Britain most doctors fiercely opposed the entry of women into the medical profession, partly because they believed that women were 'too emotional' to do such important work.

In the 1860s there were signs of a change in society's attitude towards women. By this time, some men were also arguing that women should be emancipated (freed), allowed to vote, and have the same rights to education and a choice of work as men. Elizabeth Garrett Anderson and Sophia Jex-Blake (see boxes) were the first women to gain medical qualifications in Britain and, in doing so, pointed the way to future developments. Women made a vital contribution to the medical services in both the First and Second World Wars and by the mid-20th century, women had made significant progress in being accepted into the medical profession. In 1975 the passing of the Sex Discrimination Act meant that jobs were open to everyone, irrespective of whether they were male or female.

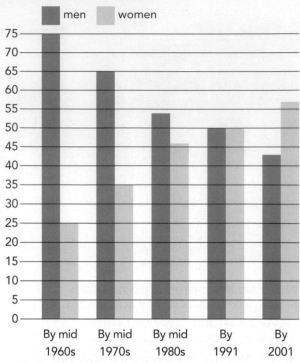

▲ The percentage proportion of women and men in medical schools in Britain.

## Source Y

### Inflexible NHS 'holds back' women doctors

Women are being held back in the race to become senior hospital doctors because of the 'working all hours' culture that remains in the NHS.

▲ An account in a newspaper, 27 June 2001, explaining how women find it difficult to get top jobs in hospitals because of the impact the excessive hours have on their family life. The report suggested that only 17 per cent of consultants in hospitals are women.

## QUESTIONS

1   What factors enabled women to progress in the medical profession?

2   What evidence is there here that there is still progress to be made?

3   Do you agree that since the Sex Discrimination Act of 1975 it has been just as easy for women to succeed in medicine as it is for men? Explain your answer.

## ELIZABETH BLACKWELL:
### The first woman doctor

Born: Bristol, 1821.

Career: Elizabeth's family emigrated to the USA. When attending a dying friend, Elizabeth was inspired to become a doctor.

She taught herself enough science to be able to study medicine, but most medical schools refused to admit a woman. After 29 refusals, she was finally accepted by a college in New York State. She graduated top of her class in 1849.

In 1853 she set up a clinic for children in New York and it was whilst working there that she caught an eye infection and had to replace her damaged eye with a glass eye.

In 1859 she travelled to Europe and met Elizabeth Garrett Anderson, who also decided to qualify as a doctor.

Died: 1910.

## ELIZABETH GARRETT ANDERSON
### (1836–1917)

Born: Whitechapel, London 1836.

Education: Her father was a rich corn and coal merchant and so Elizabeth received a good education at boarding school. In 1859 she met Elizabeth Blackwell and became convinced that she wanted a career in medicine. At first her parents disapproved, but eventually her father supported her efforts to become Britain's first female doctor.

Between 1861 and 1865 she applied to every college and hospital to train as a doctor, but was refused entry.

Career: Elizabeth became a nurse at Middlesex Hospital, and began attending lectures for male trainee doctors. After they complained she was forbidden to attend.

In 1865 she discovered that the Society of Apothecaries did not specifically ban women from taking their examinations. So she studied privately and passed their examinations. She was now qualified to be a doctor and her father paid for her to be in practice. Later she went to the University of Paris where she passed a degree in medicine (though the British Medical Register did not recognise the degree).

In 1882 she opened the New Hospital for Women in London and in 1883 became Dean of the London School of Medicine for Women. After her retirement in 1902 she was elected mayor of Aldeburgh, the first woman mayor in England.

Died: 1917.

## SOPHIA JEX-BLAKE
### (1840–1912)

Born: Hastings, 1840

Education: Sophia was the daughter of a leading physician, but he had very traditional views about women's education and did not approve of her attending university. However, he did eventually relent and Sophie became a tutor in mathematics and toured Europe and the USA teaching mathematics.

Career: In 1869 she decided that she wanted to be a doctor and persuaded Edinburgh University to allow her and three other women to be taught in separate classes from men. But after complaints from the men, the university said that it could not award degrees to women. Sophie took the university to court, but lost her case.

She took the case to parliament and eventually a law was passed in 1875 making it legal to award degrees to women. However, Sophie herself took a medical degree in Berne, Switzerland and later qualified as a doctor in Ireland.

She founded the London School of Medicine for Women in 1874.

Died: 1912.

## Source 1

▲ 'Operation Madness', a cartoon from the 1870s.

## Source 2

With the introduction of anaesthesia surgeons were free to try operations which before had been beyond them…There was some danger before the introduction of antiseptics that the risk of infection was increased.

▲ Richard Shryock, *The Development of Modern Medicine*, 1948.

## Source 3

A system of washing is much better [than carbolic spray]. I fill the abdomen with warm water and wash all the organs. The water is plain unfiltered tap water and has not been boiled.

▲ Lawson Tait, a well known surgeon in 1882, describing how operations could be successfully carried out without using antiseptics.

1 Look at Source 1.

  a What is the message of this cartoon?

  b Why do you think it was published at this time?

  c Do you think it provides reliable evidence about the impact of anaesthetics?

  Explain your answer.

2 Read Sources 2 and 3.

  a Why did it take until the late-19th century for anaesthetics and antiseptics to be widely introduced into surgery?

  b How far do these two sources explain why there was opposition to the introduction of anaesthetics and antiseptics.

3 Which do you think was the more important development in the history of surgery, anaesthetics or antiseptics? Explain your answer.

# 12.6 Exercise – nursing in the 19th century

## Background information

During the second half of the 19th century a number of important changes were made in the way that nurses were trained. Much of the credit for these changes has been given to Florence Nightingale, although other people, such as Mary Seacole, played an important part too. Just how much difference did these changes make to the standard of nursing in Britain?

## Source 1

I do not agree that the nursing establishments of our hospitals are inefficient, or that they are likely to be improved by any special institution for training. Nurses are in much the same position as housemaids and require little training or teaching beyond that of poultice-making (such skill is easily acquired), the enforcement of cleanliness and the attention to patients' needs. This proposed hospital nurse training scheme has not met with the support of the medical profession.

▲ J.F. South, President of the Royal College of Surgeons, commenting in 1851 on a proposal to set up a training school for nurses.

## Source 2

They are sexually, constitutionally and mentally unfitted for the hard and unending work, and for the heavy responsibilities of general medical and surgical practice. Women might become midwives, but in an inferior position of responsibility as a rule. I know of no great discovery changing the boundaries of scientific knowledge that owes its existence to a woman. What right have women to claim mental equality to men?

▲ An extract from an article about the role of women in medicine. It was written by a male doctor in the medical journal, *The Lancet*, in 1870.

## Source 3

You are expected to become skilful:

1 In the dressing of blisters, sores, wounds and applying poultices and dressings.

2 In the application of leeches, externally and internally.

3 In the management of helpless patients, i.e. moving, changing, cleanliness, preventing and dressing bed sores.

4 You are required to attend at operations.

5 To be competent to cook gruel, arrowfoot, egg flip puddings, drinks for the sick.

▲ Part of the instructions to newly trained nurses at Florence Nightingale's School for Nurses at St Thomas's Hospital in 1862.

1 Read Source 1. The author of this source was a senior member of the medical profession. Does this mean that a historian studying the history of medicine should take particular note of what he says? Explain your answer.

2 Read Source 2. How useful is this source to a historian studying the history of medicine? Explain your answer.

3 Read Source 3. Why do you think Florence Nightingale thought it necessary to give such precise instructions to the nurses?

4 Look at Source V on page 116. How reliable do you think this source is as evidence of Florence Nightingale's work in the Crimea? Explain your answer.

# CHAPTER 13

# DEVELOPMENTS IN PUBLIC HEALTH

## 13.1 Public health in Britain before 1700

Public health practices in Britain have varied widely, depending on where people lived and who was running the country.

Before the Roman invasion and settlement of Britain, begun in AD 43 by order of the Emperor Claudius, the people of Britain lived in tribal groups in small settlements. They were not, as many Romans felt, savages, but they did not live like the Romans. Their ideas about hygiene were different – they washed infrequently and were less careful about disposing of waste, including sewage. They had not made the connection between cleanliness and good health that the Romans had made.

### Roman Britain
The Romans had a very practical outlook on public health (see pages 32–6). When they occupied Britain, they brought their ideas about keeping clean and sewage disposal with them. However, not everyone in Britain put these ideas into practice.

Roman towns, such as Bath, had public baths, sewage disposal and clean water supplies. The people who lived in these towns benefited from this. Roman villas had baths, piped water, toilets and systems of drains and sewers. However, in those parts of Britain that had not been Romanized, for example in the Welsh countryside, people did not change their attitudes to hygiene. From AD 244 Roman control broke down, as Britain was on the edge of the Roman Empire and was one of the first places abandoned as the empire crumbled. After the Romans had gone, most of the changes they had brought, including public health measures, fell out of use.

### The Middle Ages
The Middle Ages in Britain is seen as the period from about AD 1000 to AD 1450.

Throughout this period the government failed to provide the piped water and drainage systems that would have improved public health, despite the fact that there was some awareness that dirt and disease were linked. Most people who saw a link suggested that the dirt and poor sanitation caused 'bad air'.

There were occasional clean-ups ordered by royal decrees or by law of the town corporation. However, most of the time sewage and rubbish piled up in the streets, especially in the towns and cities. The other common place for disposing of sewage and rubbish was the river – the same river that people then used for cooking and brewing. The way that people treated their waste meant that various diseases sprang up and spread rapidly. These included diseases carried in polluted water and the Black Death (see pages 55–8).

## Source A

The latrine near the Moor, outside the city walls, is badly maintained. Many sicknesses and other intolerable ills arise from the horrible, corrupt and infected atmosphere coming from this latrine.

▲ This complaint, made in 1415, resulted in the public toilets being demolished. They were re-built over the nearby Walbrook stream, which fed into the River Thames.

▼ In the Middle Ages people often built toilets out over the street or between buildings, like this one.

## Source B

## Early Modern public health

As the Middle Ages moved into the Early Modern period (1450–1700) towns and cities began to grow rapidly. London's population rose from about 60,000 in 1520 to about 200,000 in 1603. In the same period Norwich's population rose from 12,000 to 15,000 and York's from 8000 to 11,000. As more people crowded into the cities, they generated more waste of all kinds. Meanwhile, public health provision and attitudes to public health hardly changed at all.

There was a general acceptance that dirty conditions could contribute to ill health, although most people believed that this was because the air became infected. However, while people agreed on the need for cleanliness, especially in the rapidly growing towns and cities, cleaning up, providing piped water and sewage pipes all cost money and it was hard for any group of people or town corporation to raise the money to improve sanitation.

## Plague again

The poor levels of sanitation, especially in the big cities, led to outbreaks of the Black Death, otherwise called the plague. In 1665 there was an especially severe outbreak.

## Source C

Their rooms are, as a rule, planned so that a through draught is impossible, which Galen especially recommends. Floors are spread with clay and then with rushes from some marsh. These are renewed from time to time, but leaving a basic layer under which fester spittle, vomit, dog's urine and men's too, dregs of beer and cast-off bits of fish, and other unspeakable kinds of filth. As the weather changes this gives out a sort of miasma which is not conducive to bodily health.

▲ Part of a letter about the conditions to be found in houses in England generally, written in 1524 by the Dutch thinker Erasmus, who was living in England at the time.

## Source D

▲ An engraving of people burying plague victims at Holy Well Mount, London, in 1665.

## Source E

If there is plague in a house, the house, and the people in it, must be shut up for a month after the last death there.

The streets are to be kept clean and all the rubbish must be raked away.

▲ Some of the laws passed in London to try to control the outbreak of the plague there in 1665.

## QUESTIONS

1  How did Roman and British ideas about the cause of disease and the need for public health measures differ during the Roman occupation of Britain?

2  a  What, if any, connection did people in the Middle Ages and the Early Modern period make between dirt and disease?

   b  Why were there no widespread moves to improve public health in the growing towns?

3  a  What precautions are the people in Source D taking to avoid catching the plague?

   b  Write down the precautions that should be taken against the plague listed in Sources D and E. Now look back at Source W on page 57. Does your list show any change in awareness about public health issues from the precautions suggested to fight the medieval plague?

From 1700 onwards Britain was caught up in the Industrial Revolution. People no longer worked making things at home or in small workshops. They worked in bigger groups, in factories. As more and more machines were invented to help the manufacturing industries, especially the cloth industry, large factories were set up. These factories needed many workers, so factory towns or villages grew rapidly. The workers, mostly badly paid, could not afford good housing. They were either crammed into old buildings, often more than one family to a room, or new houses were built for them as cheaply as possible. Little provision was made for fresh water or sewage disposal. The government had a policy of *laissez-faire*. This means that they were not prepared to interfere with how people lived their lives, or their working and living conditions.

Town houses were often built on a back-to-back system. Sometimes they were built round a courtyard. These, like the roads, were unpaved and became muddy and contaminated with sewage. Houses were **verminous**, badly ventilated and overcrowded. Waste was piled in the courtyard or thrown into streams. Wells and watercourses quickly became polluted.

Industry made problems worse. Factory chimneys belched smoke and fumes into the air and their waste products polluted the rivers.

| THE GROWTH OF TOWNS 1801–1901 (in thousands) | | | |
|---|---|---|---|
| City | 1801 | 1851 | 1901 |
| Birmingham | 71 | 233 | 523 |
| Bradford | 13 | 104 | 280 |
| Leeds | 53 | 172 | 429 |
| Liverpool | 82 | 376 | 704 |
| Manchester | 70 | 303 | 645 |
| Newcastle | 33 | 88 | 247 |
| Nottingham | 29 | 57 | 240 |
| Sheffield | 46 | 135 | 407 |

## Source F

Alfred and Beckwith Row consist of a number of buildings, each of which is divided into two houses, one back and the other front. These houses are surrounded by a broad open drain in a filthy condition. The houses have common, open privies [toilets] which are in the most offensive condition. In one house I found six persons occupying a very small room, two in bed, ill with fever. In the room above this were two more persons in one bed, ill with fever. In this same room a woman was carrying out the process of silk weaving.

▲ Living conditions in Bethnall Green, London, as described by Dr Thomas Southwood-Smith in 1838.

▼ A view of Manchester looking from the London and North-Western railway, about 1854.

## Source G

## Disease

Bad living conditions meant that infectious diseases spread easily. The smallpox scourge of the 18th century was accompanied by tuberculosis, influenza and 'fever'. The fevers were typhoid, spread through dirty water, and typhus that was spread by the bites of body lice, which most people had because of poor personal hygiene.

These endemic diseases, which were always present in the population, were joined, in 1831–2, by a new epidemic, a disease which finally reached Britain and suddenly infected large numbers of people. This was cholera, which had been spreading across Europe from China and India since the beginning of the century.

Cholera is caused by a germ that attacks the intestines and leads to diarrhoea, vomiting, cramps, fever and death. The disease is spread through water that is infected by sewage from the victims. Cholera was first known to have entered Britain when William Sproat, a sailor, died in the port of Sunderland.

Doctors at the time had no idea what caused cholera or how to cure it. In some places barrels of tar were burnt in the streets to try to ward off 'poisonous miasmas', invisible gases that were thought to be the cause of disease. The disease spread rapidly and so many people died that the government was forced to act. Instructions were given about the immediate burial of the dead and the depth of burial.

By the end of 1832, most places in Britain had been affected by cholera and over 21,000 people had died. Then the disease seemed to die out and the boards of health that had been set up to combat it were abolished. Cholera was to return, however, in 1848, 1854 and 1866.

▲ Washing a cholera victim's bedclothes in the Mill Stream in Exeter, 1832. The stream being used was also the main source of drinking water for the city.

## Source I

Dwellings are occupied by from five to fifteen families huddled together in dirty rooms. There are slaughter houses in Butcher Row with putrid heaps of offal. Pigs are kept in large numbers. Poultry are kept in cellars and outhouses. There are dung-heaps everywhere.

▲ From *The History of the Cholera in Exeter in 1832*, written by Dr Thomas Shapter, in 1841.

## Source J

▶ A memorial to 420 cholera victims in Dumfries, Scotland, 1832.

## Edwin Chadwick and public health

The crisis brought about by the cholera epidemic of 1832 prompted the government to act. Edwin Chadwick published the *Report on the Sanitary Condition of the Labouring Population of Great Britain* in 1842. It contained evidence from doctors involved in the workings of the **Poor Law** all over the country. The information it contained about the squalor in which many working people lived and worked shocked and horrified the wealthy classes. When taken together with statistics about birth and death compiled by William Farr, from 1839, a picture was built up that showed that something needed to be done about public health in Britain.

Chadwick was convinced that sickness was the cause of poverty. He was supported by the findings of Dr Southwood Smith who, in 1838, found 14,000 cases of fever among the poor of Whitechapel, London.

## Source K

In one part of Market Street is a dunghill. Yet it is too large to be called a dunghill. I do not overestimate its size when I say that it contains 100 cubic yards [76 cubic metres] of impure filth which has been collected from all parts of the town. It is never removed. It is the main supply of a person who deals in dung. He sells it by the cart full. To please his customers he holds some back as the older the filth, the higher the price. The moisture oozes through the wall and over the pavement. This place is horrible, with swarms of flies which give a strong taste of the dunghill to any food left uncovered.

▲ A description of conditions in Greenock, Scotland, by Dr Laurie. It was included in Chadwick's 1842 Report to Parliament.

## Source L

## EDWIN CHADWICK
### 1800–90

Chadwick believed that all laws should be useful and efficient. He first worked as a lawyer but, in 1832, he became a civil servant when he helped to investigate the Poor Laws. In 1838 he was given permission to inquire into the living conditions of the poor in the East End of London. In 1840 he began a national investigation of living conditions and, in 1842, published his *Report on the Sanitary Condition of the Labouring Population*. This revealed the terrible conditions in the towns and shocked the nation. Chadwick argued that if the towns were cleaner, there would be less disease and people would not need to take time off work. As a result, fewer people would need poor relief and this would save the ratepayers money. His work inspired the sanitary reform movement.

Chadwick said that Parliament should pass legislation to improve sewage disposal and water supplies. Although he was hard working and intelligent, Chadwick could often be argumentative and tactless. He was 'pensioned off' by the government in 1854.

◀ Not even the most privileged could escape disease. This painting, dating from about 1862, shows the last moments of Prince Albert, Queen Victoria's husband. He died of typhoid fever in 1861, caught from the drains of Windsor Castle.

## The sanitary reform movement

Public health reform was slow to happen. Chadwick's 1842 report, however, did spark off a fierce debate about cleaning up the towns. Supporters of reform became known as the 'Clean Party'. In 1844 the Health of Towns Association was set up to campaign for healthier living conditions. Local branches of the Association were set up across the country. Each produced evidence of filthy streets, lack of sewage facilities and inadequate supplies of fresh water. The Association called for an Act of Parliament.

In 1847 a Public Health Bill was finally introduced into Parliament. It was strongly opposed by a group of MPs who were nicknamed the 'Dirty Party'. They believed in *laissez-faire* and argued that it was not the government's responsibility to clean up the towns. Furthermore, cleaning up the towns would cost too much money and make the government too powerful. The poor were often looked down on and it was thought they should try and help themselves. The poor did not have votes, so why should the wealthy try to help? Although Chadwick's report clearly showed that there was a connection between dirty living conditions and disease, no one knew exactly what caused these diseases.

Then, in 1848, cholera struck again and MPs voted in favour of the Bill which became the first Public Health Act.

| The First Public Health Act 1848 |
| --- |
| Central Board of Health in London to sit for five years. |
| Local Boards of Health *could* be set up in towns if 10% of the rate payers agreed. These boards had the power to improve water supply and sewage disposals. They took over from private companies and individuals. |
| The Act was not compulsory. It was not fully applied across the whole country. |

▲ **The terms of the first Public Health Act, 1848.**

## Source M

Epidemic disease amongst the labouring classes is caused by atmospheric impurities produced by decomposing animal and vegetable substances, by damp and filth, and overcrowded dwellings. The annual loss of life is greater than the loss from death or wounds in any wars in modern times. The most important and practical measures are drainage, refuse removal and the improvement of water supplies. This expense would be a financial gain by lessening the cost of sickness and death. To prevent disease it would be efficient to appoint a district medical officer.

▲ **Chadwick's main conclusions from the Report of 1842.**

## Source N

The chief theme of the speakers in opposition to the plan related to saving the pockets of the ratepayers. Their idea was calculated more to save an outlay of money than to ensure efficiency. The sewers were to discharge into the river nearby thus continuing the pollution.

▲ **Opposition to a new sewerage scheme in Leeds described by James Smith in his *Report on the Condition of the Town of Leeds*, 1844.**

## QUESTIONS

1 What public health problems resulted from the Industrial Revolution?

2 What effects did the cholera epidemic of 1831–2 have?

3 What motives did Edwin Chadwick have for trying to improve public health?

4 Why was there opposition to reform during the 1840s?

5 Why was the first Public Health Act eventually passed in 1848?

### The impact of the 1848 Public Health Act

The 1848 Act brought only limited improvements. Under the Act, local health boards, were set up in only 182 towns. As a result, sewage disposal and water supplies were improved in some of these places.

In 1854 those who were opposed to the Central Board of Health in London, were able to bring it to an end. Many water companies, landlords and builders had hated its very existence. Others still firmly believed that it was wrong for the government to interfere in people's private lives. *The Times* said, 'We prefer to take our chance of cholera and the rest than be bullied into health'. There was also bad feeling between Edwin Chadwick and the medical profession. Chadwick thought that preventing the environment from becoming filthy was the key to a healthy nation. Thus, he emphasized the need for clean water supplies and good sanitation. He did not appreciate that curative measures such as good doctors and hospitals also had a part to play. Meanwhile in September 1854, Dr John Snow had deduced that water was responsible for the spread of cholera when he plotted the victims of the disease in Broad Street, London, and found they used water from the same local pump. He removed the handle of the pump and the disease disappeared. In 1858 public health came under the control of the Privy Council and Sir John Simon, a surgeon, was made the Medical Officer of Health. He believed that public health involved both preventative and curative measures.

### Further government measures

By the mid 1860s, the government realized that it would have to become more consistently involved in providing public health. A number of factors brought about this change of attitude (see diagram).

In 1869 Simon persuaded the government to set up the Royal Sanitary Commission. It found that the provision of clean water was still very patchy and recommended that laws should be made which were 'uniform, universal and imperative'. The government responded by forming the Local Government Board (1871) to oversee the administration of public health. The 1872 Public Health Act divided the country into 'sanitary areas' each with a medical officer of health. In 1875 Benjamin Disraeli's Conservative government passed a second Public Health Act and the Artisans' Dwellings Act – which together formed the most wide-reaching legislation to date.

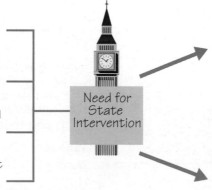

- Further cholera outbreaks in 1854 and 1866 frighten the authorities once more.

- In 1854 Dr John Snow showed that cholera was spread by contaminated water.

- In 1864 Louis Pasteur demonstrated the germ theory of disease. Need for cleanliness became clear.

- By the 1870s statistics showed that poor living conditions and disease were connected.

**Need for State Intervention**

**1875 Second Public Health Act**
- brought together all previous laws under one act.
- councils compelled to provide street lighting, clean water, drainage, and sewage disposal.
- councils had to employ medical inspectors.

**1875 Artisans' Dwellings Act**
- councils given power to buy up areas of slum housing, knock them down and build new houses.
- few councils took advantage.

▲ **Factors leading to state intervention into public health.**

## OCTAVIA HILL

Octavia Hill was born in 1838. Her parents and grandparents were involved in charity work, so Octavia and her sisters naturally joined in. In 1853 Octavia started to work with a group of women called the Ladies' Guild. She taught in a ragged school. This was the first instance of her working with the poor. By 1858 she and her sister had set up their own school. Working in poor areas showed her how appalling the housing conditions of the poor were. She began to plan how they could be improved. In 1865 she managed to raise enough money to buy the leases of three houses. She repaired them, collected the rent regularly and got to know the tenants. She made sure that tenants did not take in lodgers – which led to severe overcrowding and the spread of infection. She got rid of the bad tenants and improved the homes for the remaining tenants, who then looked after the houses.

Octavia's scheme was a success. Her tenants cared for their homes and paid the rent on time. This quickly paid off the costs of improvements. Everyone was better off. Soon many people, from ordinary people to the Church of England, were paying Octavia to manage their properties for them. She used the money she made on this to buy up more houses for the poor. People began to think that Octavia talked a lot of sense about how to help the poor. In 1869 she helped to set up the Charity Organization Society and also pushed for open spaces in all cities for the use of everyone, especially the poor. She felt that this would help to stop houses being crowded together and give the poor places where they could exercise in the open air. Both these things would be good for their health. She campaigned for better conditions for the poor until her death in 1912.

## JOHN SNOW
### AND CHOLERA

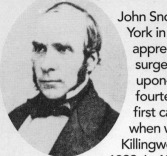

John Snow was born in York in 1813 and was apprenticed to a surgeon in Newcastle-upon-Tyne at the age of fourteen. He saw his first cases of cholera when working at Killingworth Colliery in 1833. In 1838 Snow travelled to London and qualified as a member of the Royal College of Surgeons. He then set up a medical practice in Soho. One of his most famous acts was to administer chloroform to Queen Victoria to ease the pain of childbirth.

During the 1848 outbreak of cholera in London, Snow spent a great deal of time investigating the causes of the disease. He discovered that in one area of London the people who caught cholera drank water which came from the Thames. In the same area some people took their water from a pump using water from fresh springs. They did not catch cholera. He set out his ideas that the disease was transmitted through water not through the air, but not everyone accepted his view.

## Source O

The state of the air which is most likely to encourage cholera is a hot, moist atmosphere. Under these conditions the unpleasant animal and vegetable refuse rots the most quickly and poisons from it are carried in greatest quantity into the blood from the lungs.

▲ A report from the new government department, the Central Board of Health. It is explaining why cholera seemed to be worse in the summer than in the winter.

DIPTHERIA.        SCROFULA.        CHOLERA.

## FATHER THAMES INTRODUCING HIS OFFSPRING TO THE FAIR CITY OF LONDON.

*(A Design for a Fresco in the New Houses of Parliament.)*

▲ A *Punch* cartoon of 1858, showing Father Thames introducing his children (diptheria, scrofula and cholera) to London.

## Source Q

In hot, dry weather the Thames becomes like a huge lake. The water level falls so that little of the river reaches the sea. Instead it receives the filth of more than 2 million inhabitants which collects there until there is enough rain to swell the water. In times of cholera the evacuations of patients join the impurities in the river.

▲ A description of the River Thames, from the 1850s.

## QUESTIONS

1  'Source P shows that many people must have agreed with Snow about the cause of cholera.' Explain whether you agree with this statement.

2  Why do you think the Board of Health (Source O) incorrectly explained that hot weather seemed to lead to increases in cholera?

Between 1886 and 1903 Charles Booth, a shipowner and social investigator, carried out a survey into living conditions in the East End of London. He published his findings in *Life and Labour of the People* in London. Booth concluded that about one-third of the people lived on incomes lower than 21s (£1.05) per week. In his opinion this was below the poverty line. They lived in sub-standard housing and had a poor diet. If they fell ill they could not afford to pay a doctor. In 1899 Seebohm Rowntree, a member of the chocolate manufacturing family, conducted his own inquiry in York. And his findings were very similar. Booth said that poverty was caused by sickness, old age, low wages and lack of employment – not laziness and drunkenness as many believed. There were no old age pensions. Old people who could not support themselves had only the workhouse to turn to. Many skilled workers could afford to pay into Friendly Societies and insure themselves against unemployment and illness. Unskilled workers, however, could not afford the subscriptions.

## Time for action

In 1902 the nation was shocked to find that 40 per cent of those that had volunteered to fight in the **Boer War** were suffering from malnutrition and diseases such as rickets, caused by poor diet. It was clear ill-health was linked to poverty and that government action was needed to raise living standards. Some Liberal MPs were concerned that people would vote for the newly formed Labour Party if they did not help the poor.

The Liberals went on to pass a wide range of reforms (see diagram). Churchill said, 'Our cause is the cause of the left out millions. We are all agreed that the state must concern itself with the care of the sick, the aged and, above all, children.'

**Source R**

▲ Slum housing in the east end of London in 1912.

| Date | Legislation |
| --- | --- |
| 1906 | **Provision of school meals** – local authorities given the power to provide free school meals. |
| 1907 | **School medical inspections.** |
| 1909 | **Old Age Pension Act** – people over 70 to receive 5s [25p] per week state pension as long as their income from other sources was not more than 12s [60p] per week. |
| 1909 | **Labour Exchanges** set up to help unemployed find work. |
| 1911 | **National Insurance Act** – two parts: <br><br>Part I: Workers in manual trades earning less than £160 per year to pay 4d [2p] per week. The employer added 3d [1½p] and the government 2d [1p]. Workers entitled to 10s [50p] per week if they were off work sick, for upto 26 weeks. Free medical treatment available from a panel doctor. <br><br>Part II: Workers, earning less than £160 per year in certain trades, together with the government and employers paid in 2¼d [1p] per week. Workers could claim 7s [35p] unemployment pay for up to 15 weeks. |

▲ Social reforms of the Liberal government 1906–14.

## How did people react to the reforms?

For the first time the state had made a co-ordinated attack on poverty. Much of the legislation, however, was not very far-reaching and Lloyd George admitted that they had only just made a start. Nevertheless there was fierce resistance to some of the measures.

To pay for old age pensions, Lloyd George introduced the People's Budget, that aimed to tax the rich to provide for the poor. The House of Lords, largely made up of wealthy landowners, refused to pass the budget. This issue forced two general elections in 1910. The Liberals were narrowly returned. The budget was then allowed through but, in 1911, the power of the House of Lords to throw out finance bills was abolished by the Parliament Act. The Labour Party said that pensions should have been payable at 65, whereas many Conservatives were of the opinion that pensions 'would profoundly weaken the moral fibre of the nation, (report in *The Times*, 17 December 1909). People who qualified for a pension, however, were thankful to 'Lord' George.

The National Insurance Act was also widely condemned. Friendly societies and private insurance companies said that they would lose business. To overcome this, Lloyd George agreed to drop proposals for pensions to be paid to orphans and widows. He also allowed the Act to be administered by private insurance companies acting as 'approved societies' on behalf of the government. The Labour Party said that workers should not have to pay any money at all into the scheme, arguing that benefits should be paid entirely from taxes. Many doctors opposed the Act. They now had to register with a panel (a local list) and would receive 6 shillings (30p) for each patient under their care. Doctors argued that this meant a loss of independence and would cause medical standards to drop. In the face of such opposition, Lloyd George had to be strong and prepared to negotiate.

## Government and social welfare 1919–39

After the First World War (1914–18) Lloyd George, by now the Prime Minister, promised to make Britain 'a country fit for heroes to live in'.

In 1919 the Ministry of Health was set up to administer all matters to do with health. This, in itself, was an important step forward as previously health came under the jurisdiction of seven different government departments. During the war, house building had been neglected so, in 1919, the new Minister for Health, Christopher Addison, passed the Housing and Town Planning Act. Under this Act the government gave local authorities a grant to help them build council houses. In 1920 the Unemployment Insurance Act extended insurance cover to all workers (except farm labourers and domestic servants) who earned less than £250 per year.

**THE GLORIOUS FIFTEENTH**

Our St. Sebastian "AND NOW, LADIES AND GENTLEMEN, AFTER THESE REFRESHING PRELIMINARIES, LET US GET TO BUSINESS."

▲ **Lloyd George had to overcome fierce opposition in steering the National Insurance Bill through Parliament. Do you think the cartoonist was a Lloyd George supporter?**

## QUESTIONS

1 Why was the Central Board of Health abolished in 1854?

2 Study the diagram on page 128. Which factor was the most important in bringing greater government involvement in public health?

3 Why did the Liberals pass a wide range of social reforms?

4 Summarize the main Acts passed by the Liberals under these headings:

   ● Acts dealing with children
   ● Acts dealing with the unemployed
   ● Acts dealing with health and sickness
   ● Acts dealing with the elderly.

5 The Liberal reforms helped many people. Why was there opposition to them at the time?

## Rising unemployment

By 1922 the economy was in trouble. There was a slump in trade and rising unemployment. The government was forced to reduce its spending on housing, education and welfare provision. Other ways had to be found of funding reforms. Neville Chamberlain, Minister of Health from 1924–9, therefore encouraged the private sector to build more houses. The Pensions Act of 1925 was also Chamberlain's work. Pensions, funded by contributions from the state, employer and worker, were introduced at the age of 65. During the 1930s there was a world depression with mass unemployment. Dealing with the unemployed was more urgent than introducing welfare measures. The government was short of money and, therefore, reluctant to finance social reforms.

Despite this some progress in social provision was made between 1919 and 1939 (see Source U). The main problem was that the welfare services were an administrative muddle. Some services were provided by the government and some by private organizations. Health care, in particular, was a 'chaotic mixture' (see diagram). Opinion was growing that the health care system needed to be reformed. The Socialist Medical Association and the trade unions said that health services should be organized by the state. Others, however, still believed that voluntary organizations and self-help had a part to play. Many thought that social welfare should be provided only for the poor. It was argued that people who had the money should pay for their own medical treatment and schooling. The Second World War (1939–45) was to change many people's attitudes to welfare provision.

## Source T

▲ This *Punch* cartoon from October 1937 portrays Neville Chamberlain as anxious to lead the way to health reforms. Chamberlain was Chancellor of the Exchequer from 1931–7. The reality was that the government was mainly concerned with the problem of unemployment caused by the Depression.

### An unco-ordinated system

**Hospitals**
- About 3,000 in Britain, 1,000 were run by voluntary funds. Hospitals unevenly spread.
- Poor people were treated in workhouse infirmaries.

**Doctors**
- Wealthy received best treatment as they could afford the fees.
- Some workers, covered by National Insurance, had panel doctors. [dependants not covered]

**Other services**
Local authorities provided:
- school medical inspectors
- ante-natal clinics
- infant-welfare centres.

▲ Health care in 1939.

## Source U

[In 1939] Britain was one of the most advanced of all countries in social provision. The majority of manual workers [but not their wives and children] were covered by social insurance schemes... The social services were complex and growing. State elementary schools and municipal hospitals were familiar landmarks. Ante-natal clinics and infant welfare centres were multiplying, and three million children received free milk in school.

▲ Paul Addison, *A New Jerusalem*, 1994.

### Slow change

During the early years of the 20th century, the Liberals had brought in a series of reforms to improve the living and working conditions of the people of Britain. During the 1920s and 1930s there had been further help for those in need through improvements in housing, unemployment benefit and pensions (see page 133).

But these were only the first steps on the road towards the establishment of the government's acceptance of its responsibility to provide help for all those in need. During the 1930s the British economy experienced great difficulties as the impact of the Wall Street Crash was felt across the world. There was no money to spend on extending government welfare services. Instead the government was struggling to raise the money to finance its existing commitments.

### The war years

In 1939 the Second World War broke out in Europe. The measures that the government took to help win the war proved very important in helping to bring about increases in social support in Britain.

- During the war there were shortages of food and the government was determined that children should be fed properly. So it ordered local education authorities to extend their provision of free school meals. Free school milk was also provided.

- Britain suffered heavy bombing during the war, particularly during the blitz of 1940–1. To cope with the casualties the government set up the Emergency Medical Service. Hospitals were put under the Ministry of Health and free treatment was provided. This arrangement proved to be very successful and people accepted that the government should be more involved in running the 'health service'.

- A most influential result of the war upon the increase of welfare provision was the programme of evacuation. Children from the inner cities were evacuated to rural areas in order to escape the air raids. The people with whom they stayed were often shocked at the filthy, deprived and badly clothed children who arrived in the towns and villages looking for new homes. Lord Chandos, who took in 31 evacuees, complained that these children regarded 'the floors and carpets as suitable places on which to relieve themselves'.

## Source V

◀ A cartoon from the *Daily Mirror* published during the Second World War. It shows 'War' providing food and vitamins to a young child.

## Source W

They were filthy; we have never seen so many children with lice and nits and lacking any knowledge of clean and hygienic habits. It seemed as if they hadn't bathed for months. Some children had dirty, septic sores all over their bodies. Many of the children were bedwetters and were not in the habit of doing anything else.

▲ An extract from a report of the Women's Institute in 1940.

## The Beveridge Report

In 1941 the government asked Sir William Beveridge, a well-known economist, to suggest ways in which the government could help the sick, the unemployed, low-paid workers and retired people. In 1942 the Beveridge Report was published. He recommended that the government should provide a welfare state 'taking charge of social security from the cradle to the grave'. In other words, it was the duty of the government to look after all members of society, not just the poor. He argued that all cities had a right to be free from the five 'giants' which could ruin peoples' lives. These were:

- want (need)
- disease
- ignorance
- squalor
- idleness.

The Beveridge Report became a best seller with over 100,000 copies sold in the first month. Members of all political parties welcomed the report, but the Prime Minister, Winston Churchill, feared that the country might not be able to afford to introduce all the measures suggested in the report. In a cabinet meeting in 1943 he asked whether 'we are committing our 45 million people to burdens beyond their capacity to bear'.

## The National Health Service

In July 1945 the Labour Party came to power, and it fell to them to introduce a Beveridge-style welfare state. **Family Allowances** and compulsory **National Insurance** for everyone were introduced in 1948. The central hub of Labour's reform programme was the National Health Service, masterminded by the Minister of Health, Aneurin Bevan. The NHS was to provide free medical treatment for everyone. It came into operation on 5 July 1948. Hospitals came under the control of the state and local authorities were to provide free services including ambulances, vaccination programmes, environmental health, maternity clinics and health visitors. Doctors, opticians and dentists provided a free service.

Source **X**

▲ A cartoon published in the *Evening Standard*, December 1949. It is called 'Right Turn'.

## SIR WILLIAM BEVERIDGE

Sir William Beveridge was born in 1879 and was educated at Oxford University. He was knighted in 1919 after the First World War and in the same year became Director of the London School of Economics. In 1937 he became Master of University College, Oxford. In 1942 he produced the famous Beveridge Report and two years later entered Parliament as a Liberal MP. In 1946 he was created the 1st Baron Beveridge of Tuggal in recognition of his part in helping to bring about the Welfare State.

## Reactions to the NHS

The NHS was received with great enthusiasm by most people. Immediately people took advantage of the free medical service. But there were also many people who were opposed to the new system. In early 1948 the British Medical Association, which represented the medical profession, carried out a survey to see what doctors thought. The results were as follows:

In favour of the NHS      4734
Opposed to the NHS      40,814

Doctors feared that the new system would give the government too much control. They would now be employed by the government and might be told where they had to practice. They could no longer charge for their services, and would be on a fixed salary. This might lead to a reduction in their income.

The Minister of Health responsible for introducing the NHS, Aneurin Bevan, was not a man to back down in the face of opposition. He had many angry discussions with the leader of the British Medical Association, Charles Hill, before agreement was reached. In the end Bevan won the doctors over by stating that they would receive a fee for each patient they registered and that they would still be able to treat private fee-paying patients if they wished. By June 1948, 92 per cent of doctors and the vast majority of hospitals had agreed to work under the NHS.

## Source Y

She went and got tested for new glasses, then she went to the chiropodist, she had her feet done. Then she went back to the doctor's because she'd been having trouble with her ears and the doctor said he would fix her up with a hearing aid.

▲ **How one old lady reacted to the NHS, quoted by Paul Addison, in** *Now the War is Over,* **1985.**

When the NHS started, oh it was fantastic. My mother and dad had been having problems with their teeth for ages, and I think they were first at the dentist, as soon as he opened. And instead of having just a few teeth out they had the complete set out. And free dentures. Thought it was wonderful.

▲ **A woman describing her reaction to the NHS.**

## QUESTIONS

1   Look at the cartoon. Do you think the cartoonist approved or disapproved of the NHS? Explain your answer.

## Source Z

▲ **A cartoon from 1948 showing Aneurin Bevan dishing out 'NHS medicine' to the doctors.**

## Problems faced by the NHS

When the NHS was set up, it aimed to provide the best possible care for everyone. This was to be paid for out of peoples' taxes and National Insurance contributions. However, two significant factors have made it increasingly difficult to provide the NHS with all the funds it needs:

- Firstly, the death rate has declined and people are living longer. So there are more people to treat.
- Secondly new cures have been found and new illnesses have developed. Some of these are very costly – for instance, transplant operations and many of the new drugs produced for illnesses such as AIDS which had not been heard of in 1948.

These two factors have led to an enormous increase in government spending on the NHS.

## Spending on the NHS 1950–2000

UK £ billion

| Year | UK £ billion |
|------|--------------|
| 1950 | 9.5 |
| 1960 | 11.5 |
| 1970 | 17.0 |
| 1980 | 26.0 |
| 1990 | 34.5 |
| 2000 | 50.0 (estimate) |
| 2002 | 65.4 (estimate) |

There has been heated debate about how to pay for the increased spending on the NHS. One way has been to increase prescription charges. Another has been to encourage people to take out private medical insurance to take the pressure off the NHS. Both of these measures have been controversial. Opponents of prescription charges say that such charges are contrary to the idea of a free NHS. Some people also argue that extending private medicine would lead to a two-tier system whereby the wealthy would receive better treatment.

A shortage of money has led to doctors and hospitals having to make some very difficult choices. Sometimes treatment is refused because of lack of money or sometimes because a patient's illness is 'self-inflicted' (for example, an illness caused by smoking). Sometimes patients have to wait so long for important operations that they die before the operation can be carried out.

The Labour government elected in 1997 took measures to try to improve the NHS. Some patients found themselves transferred to other countries, such as France, to have operations, rather than suffer a long wait in Britain. In March 2002 the Chancellor of the Exchequer, Gordon Brown, introduced a budget which increased National Insurance contributions. He said that he wanted to use the income to increase spending on the NHS by 7.4 per cent a year, so as to reach £105.6 billion in 2007–8.

## Vaccination programmes

After 1948 the drive to improve the population's personal health was stepped up. Vaccination programmes, funded by the state, were put in place for all children. In 1954 Jonas Salk produced an effective vaccine against polio, a terrifying disease which, at its worst, could cause paralysis; it struck particularly at young people. In 1960 Albert Sabin produced an improved vaccine which could be taken orally on a sugar lump.

In 1948 the World Health Organization (WHO), an agency of the United Nations, was set up. One of its aims is to encourage vaccination programmes on a global scale. Advances have been made and today eight out of every ten children have been vaccinated against the major killer diseases.

In recent times, however, there have been doubts amongst some doctors about the safety of certain vaccines. In Britain it has been common practice to give young children a 'three-in-one' vaccination against mumps, measles and rubella. Some people argue that this has caused autism in a small number of children and so the numbers of children being vaccinated have dropped. Other doctors argue that this will lead to an increase in the individual diseases, often with tragic consequences.

## Alternative medicine

Developments in drugs have meant that we can often provide a pill or potion which will bring about a rapid cure to an illness or disease. Although this seems successful, in recent times some people have begun to question the wisdom of such an approach. They argue that continually bombarding the body with strong drugs cannot be beneficial in the long term. As our bodies develop immunity to drugs, so we have to find even stronger ones to cure the problem. Strong drugs can have very unpleasant side effects or led to addiction. Critics talk of a 'valium society' where problems with lifestyle are solved by regularly taking anti-depressants.

In the 21st century there is an increasing interest in maintaining both physical and mental health. This has led many people to consider whether a better approach to medicine is to look at the general health of the patient as a whole, not just individual symptoms. Consequently a number of different approaches to medicine have become increasingly popular. Since they are alternatives to modern 'scientific' medicine, they have generally been labelled 'alternative medicine'.

- One of the fastest growing 'alternative approaches' is the ancient practice of **herbal medicine**. Instead of taking drugs, people look to natural cures from herbs.
- **Hypnotherapy** is also increasing in popularity and is related to **psychotherapy** in that they both try to treat problems of the mind rather than the body. Spiritual or faith healing, which often involves 'the laying on of hands' is also sometimes used. Sceptics dismiss this approach as unscientific or even 'bogus', yet in a recent survey 90 per cent of people using faith healing were satisfied with its effects.

- **Acupuncture** was first developed in China 4000 years ago and involves inserting needles into pressure points in the body. These needles release blocked energy. Acupuncture has proved effective for migraines and as an anaesthetic during surgery.
- **Homeopathy** is based on the theory that 'like cures like'. A diluted substance similar to the original illness is taken and this provokes the body into providing its own natural cure.

These are just some of the many types of alternative medical approaches available. You may want to find out more about other practices, such as chiropractic, osteopathy, reflexology and aromatherapy.

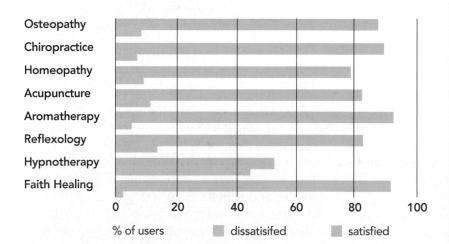

▲ The results of a recent survey by the consumer magazine, *Which?* It shows that people who had tried alternative treatments mainly regarded them as successful.

## QUESTIONS

1 What part did the following factors play in the introduction of a welfare state after 1945?

- the work of the Liberal government, 1906–14
- changing social attitudes
- the 1942 Beveridge Report
- Labour's election victory in 1945?

2 Explain the reactions of ordinary people to the setting up of the NHS.

3 'Doctors opposed the introduction of the NHS because they were selfish.' Explain whether you agree with this statement.

## Source 1

▲ Barrels of tar being burned in the streets of Exeter as a remedy for cholera, during the epidemic of 1831–2.

1 Burning barrels of tar will not stop diseases like cholera from spreading. Why, then, did many town councils order this to be done during the cholera epidemic of 1831–2?

2 Why were there four outbreaks of cholera between 1831 and 1866?

3 The first Act of Parliament to tackle the problems of public health effectively was the Public Health Act of 1875 (Source 3). Why was this Act so long delayed?

4 Which of the events shown in Source 3 did the most to bring about a Welfare State in Britain? Explain your answer.

## Source 2

▲ A view of industrial Sheffield in the mid-19th century.

## Source 3

**Some events which improved health and welfare in Britain**

**1875** Second Public Health Act passed. Local councils were made to provide fresh water and sanitation.

**1909** The first old age pensions were paid.

**1942** The Beveridge Report said that the government should look after its citizens from 'the cradle to the grave'.

**1948** The National Health Service came into being – free medical care for everyone.

▲ From a modern history book.

# CHAPTER 14

# CONCLUSION: CHANGE, CONCEPTS AND FACTORS

As we have now seen, the history of medicine is not one of steady progress. It is a story where the rate of change varies. At some times change was very rapid, at others very slow. Sometimes things changed for the better, at other times they got worse. We have looked at different aspects of medicine through time:

● *understanding about the cause and cure of disease*
● *anatomy*
● *surgery*
● *public health and prevention of disease*
● *surgeons, doctors and nurses – the development of a medical profession.*

These different aspects of medicine have developed at different rates. For example, the standards of public health provision in British towns at the height of the Roman Empire was probably better than it was from the fall of the empire until 1850, yet the understanding of the cause and cure of disease was greater from the middle of the 16th century than in Roman times.

If you were considering how understanding of the cause and cure of disease rose and fell during the period covered in this book, you might make a list which looked like this:

1  There was notable progress in Greece around the time of Hippocrates.
2  There was then very gradual improvement through to the late Roman Empire.
3  There was a sharp fall in standards during the Dark Ages.
4  This was followed by a slow rise in standards, which got faster following the establishment of medical schools in the Middle Ages.

5  There was another fast improvement during the Renaissance.
6  This was followed by a further period of gradual improvement until the discovery of the germ theory.
7  Since the acceptance of the germ theory our knowledge has increased rapidly, with the identification of disease-causing microbes and the development of vaccines and drugs.

What would be on your list if you made one for:

● public health
● anatomy
● training of doctors and nurses?

Throughout your study of the history of medicine you have been using factors and concepts to help you understand what happened and why. The history of medicine presents you with an enormous amount of information. Factors and concepts give you the tools to shape this information into patterns.

## Concepts
The most important concepts for you to discuss are:

*Development and change:* where a new idea builds on work that has gone before, or strikes off in different directions.

*Progress and regress:* where things can either get better or worse.

*The rate of change:* which is variable – sometimes things change very quickly, and other times very slowly or not at all.

*Trends and turning points:* trends take place over a long time and are made up of a number of related developments. Turning points are sudden changes which produce a change in direction.

Can you find examples of each of the concepts above from the three main periods you have studied:

- Ancient (up to the fall of the Roman Empire)
- 500 AD – 1800 AD
- Modern (from 1800 onwards)?

## Factors

Factors and concepts do not work in isolation from each other. You can find a whole range of factors working with each concept. For example:

*Chance:* this can be seen to have been a key factor in bringing about both progress and regress.

Chance caused regress when the Minoan civilization of Crete was destroyed and the advances the Minoans had made in sanitation and drainage were lost to the Mediterranean world.

Chance was an equally important factor in progress when Paré ran out of boiling oil to use on gunshot wounds after a battle in 1537. He was forced to try a new treatment, which he would not otherwise have tried, and found it worked much better than the treatment with boiling oil.

Both these cases illustrate chance – nobody planned that these events should happen, or decided they would be a good thing.

*War:* this can be shown to have increased the rate of change.

The money put into medical development during the Second World War, and the new treatments developed due to the pressure of large numbers of casualties, resulted in changes including the mass-production of penicillin and the development of plastic surgery by Archibald McIndoe.

Six years of war saw astonishing progress, but war also had negative effects on medicine. The collapse of the Roman Empire followed military defeat. This led to regress, most obviously in public health in most of Europe.

*Religion:* has also been a factor in both progress and regress.

In the Middle Ages, from 1300 onwards, the Church had forbidden the boiling of bodies to produce skeletons for study by doctors and anatomists.

The lack of knowledge about the skeleton this caused kept medieval anatomy below the standards that had been achieved by Galen and his contemporaries in the Roman Empire. Earlier, religion had helped medicine progress through the practice of mummification in Egypt which ensured doctors had some knowledge of human anatomy.

You may well be asked in your exam to provide examples of how each of these factors helped or hindered medical developments. You may also have to talk about how the factors worked together. So be prepared! Make sure you have all the other factors covered too. These are:

- science and technology
- communications
- the work of Individuals
- government.

# GLOSSARY

**agar** a jelly prepared from seaweed for bacteria to grow on for use in experiments.

**AIDS** Acquired Immune Deficiency Syndrome – a virus which attacks the immune system leaving the sufferer very open to infection.

**anaesthetics** drugs given to a patient to make surgery pain free.

**antibiotic** drug derived from a living organism, such as fungi, which would kill bacteria, or prevent it from growing.

**antibody** a defensive substance produced in the body to neutralize a foreign micro-organism or poison.

**antisepsis** the use of antiseptics (first carbolic acid) to kill germs.

**arsenic** a chemical element which, though poisonous, is sometimes used in minute quantities in medicines.

**ascendant** the star or planet rising at the time of a person's birth.

**asepsis** sterilising the air, the clothing and tools of doctors in the operating room to remove the risk of germs.

**astrology** the study of the influence of the stars and planets on human events.

**astronomy** the study of stars, planets and other objects in space.

**attenuation** thinning something out or weakening it. In medicine attenuation refers to the idea of weakening a germ, so it loses its effectiveness.

**bacillus** any bacterium (microscopic plant) which causes disease.

**barber-surgeons** barbers who also performed minor surgery and dentistry. They were mainly used by the poor.

**bezoar stone** stony mass found in the stomach of goats, antelopes, llama, etc., previously thought to be an antidote to all poisons.

**Boer War** a war fought in 1899–1902 between the small Dutch republics in South Africa and the British who saw all of South Africa as part of the British Empire.

**caesarean section** delivery of a child by cutting open the mother's abdomen.

**caliph** a Muslim leader during the time of the Islamic Empire.

**cautery** a method of treating amputated limbs or wounds by burning them with hot iron or oil to prevent infection and seal the wound.

**Christendom** all Christians.

**circulating** going round; Harvey's understanding of blood circulation was of enormous importance to medical development.

**clone** to make an exact copy (a genetically identical copy) of cells or an organism. In recent years scientists have been able to clone animals such as sheep.

**colycynth** a kind of cucumber.

**Crusades** military expeditions in the name of Christianity to recover the Holy Land from Muslims.

**distillation** converting liquid into vapour by heating it and then condensing it again into droplets. This was done either to extract a component of the liquid or to purify it.

**empirical** relying on experience or observation.

**Family Allowance** an amount of money given weekly by the state for the support of children.

**fibre optics** extremely thin glass fibres which are used in optical instruments; their flexibility and use of maximum light make them ideally suited for use in very inaccessible places.

**herbal medicine** medical remedies made only from plant material such as leaves, roots and bark.

**hypnotherapy** the treatment of a patient when hypnotised. The hypnotherapist asks questions and makes suggestions to the patient after putting the patient into a relaxed, dreamlike state.

**Islam** the Muslim world.

**immune** resistant to disease.

**National Insurance** a system of compulsory insurance, paid for by weekly contributions by employers and employees, to pay for benefits to the sick, retired and unemployed.

**Nationalism** the belief in striving after the unity, independence, interests or domination of a nation.

**natural** something which is physical, observable and of this world.

**opium** a drug derived from the white poppy producing sleepiness, numbness, euphoria or loss of memory.

**pilgrimage** a journey to a shrine or holy place.

**plague** there are two main forms of plague: bubonic (characterised by buboes or lumps), spread by flea bites; and pneumonic (respiratory), spread by coughing or sneezing.

**Poor Law** laws relating to the support of the poor.

**psychotherapy** the treatment of individuals, couples or groups in which painful emotions and experiences are discussed with a qualified psychotherapist. The process of talking about how the patient thinks and feels is thought to help reduce painful feelings and lead to greater self-confidence.

**progress** moving forward, often implying improvement.

**rational** ruled by reason.

**regress** going backwards, often implying getting worse.

**Renaissance** means 'rebirth'. The period of the Renaissance marked the transition from medieval to modern history in the 14th century, and was a time when the arts and sciences flourished.

**solid cultures** experimentally grown bacteria in nutritive solid substances.

**supernatural** outside the world as we know it, sometimes involving gods, spirits and unknown forces.

**suture** a surgeon's stitch.

**thalidomide** a drug, withdrawn in 1961 because it was found to cause malformation in the foetus if taken during pregnancy.

**tracheotomy** an operation which involves cutting into the trachea or windpipe.

**verminous** to be infested with obnoxious insects such as fleas and lice, and troublesome animals such as mice or rats.